FOUL DEEDS AND SUSPICIOUS DEATHS IN BARNET, FINCHLEY AND HENDON

TRUE CRIME FROM WHARNCLIFFE

Foul Deeds and Suspicious Deaths Series

Barking, Dagenham & Chadwell Heath
Barnsley
Bath
Bedford
Birmingham
Black Country
Blackburn and Hyndburn
Bolton
Bradford
Brighton
Bristol
Cambridge
Carlisle
Chesterfield
Colchester
Coventry
Croydon
Derby
Dublin
Durham
Ealing
Folkestone and Dover
Grimsby
Guernsey
Guildford
Halifax
Hampstead, Holborn and St Pancras
Huddersfield
Hull

Leeds
Leicester
Lewisham and Deptford
Liverpool
London's East End
London's West End
Manchester
Mansfield
More Foul Deeds Birmingham
More Foul Deeds Chesterfield
More Foul Deeds Wakefield
Newcastle
Newport
Norfolk
Northampton
Nottingham
Oxfordshire
Pontefract and Castleford
Portsmouth
Rotherham
Scunthorpe
Southend-on-Sea
Staffordshire and The Potteries
Stratford and South Warwickshire
Tees
Warwickshire
Wigan
York

OTHER TRUE CRIME BOOKS FROM WHARNCLIFFE

A-Z of Yorkshire Murder
Black Barnsley
Brighton Crime and Vice 1800-2000
Durham Executions
Essex Murders
Executions & Hangings in Newcastle
   and Morpeth
Norfolk Mayhem and Murder

Norwich Murders
Strangeways Hanged
The A-Z of London Murders
Unsolved Murders in Victorian and
   Edwardian London
Unsolved Norfolk Murders
Unsolved Yorkshire Murders
Yorkshire's Murderous Women

Please contact us via any of the methods below for more information or a catalogue.

WHARNCLIFFE BOOKS

47 Church Street – Barnsley – South Yorkshire – S70 2AS
Tel: 01226 734555 – 734222 Fax: 01226 – 734438
E-mail: enquiries@pen-and-sword.co.uk
Website: www.wharncliffebooks.co.uk

Foul Deeds & Suspicious Deaths in

BARNET, FINCHLEY AND HENDON

NICK PAPADIMITRIOU

To Reg Long

First published in Great Britain in 2009 by
Wharncliffe Books
an imprint of
Pen & Sword Books Ltd
47 Church Street
Barnsley
South Yorkshire
S70 2AS

Copyright © Nick Papadimitriou 2009

ISBN 978 1 84563 064 5

Typeset in 11/13pt Plantin by
Mac Style, Beverley, East Yorkshire

Printed and bound in the UK by
CPI

Pen & Sword Books Ltd incorporates the imprints of Pen & Sword
Aviation, Pen & Sword Maritime, Pen & Sword Military, Wharncliffe Local
History, Pen and Sword Select, Pen and Sword Military Classics and
Leo Cooper.

For a complete list of Pen & Sword titles please contact
PEN & SWORD BOOKS LIMITED
47 Church Street, Barnsley, South Yorkshire, S70 2AS, England
E-mail: enquiries@pen-and-sword.co.uk
Website: www.pen-and-sword.co.uk

Contents

Preface & Acknowledgements   6

Introduction   7

Part One   Early Cases   15

Chapter 1   From the Middlesex Court Rolls, c.1500–1700   13

Chapter 2   A Case of Witchcraft, 1615   17

Chapter 3   The Man Who Murdered Himself, 1684   21

Part Two   Modern Times   25

Chapter 4   Death in Coppett's Wood, 1884   25

Chapter 5   Who Killed Lydia Hill? 1895   32

Chapter 6   The College Farm Murder, 1898   39

Chapter 7   The Girl in the Silkstream, 1909   45

Chapter 8   A Tale of Two Sweethearts, 1911   51

Chapter 9   A Circus Entrepreneur takes his Final Bow, 1911   60

Chapter 10   The West Hendon Shootings, 1911 & 1913   65

Chapter 11   The Hendon Wine Shop Murder, 1919   76

Chapter 12   'She Made Me Do It,' 1920   86

Chapter 13   He Tried to Disappear, 1930   99

Chapter 14   Crack-up   105

Chapter 15   The Rogues of Clay Lane, 1931   115

Chapter 16   The Stabbing of a Chocolate Girl, 1936   124

Chapter 17   An Unhappy Suburb, 1938-39   133

Chapter 18   He Wanted it All, 1937   138

Chapter 19   Shot at Point-blank Range, 1941   144

Chapter 20   A Soldier Returns Home, 1942   154

Chapter 21   The Body in the Marshes, 1949   158

Chapter 22   A Case of Post-war Sleaze, 1949   168

Chapter 23   A Doctor Dies in Colindale, 1975   177

Chapter 24   The Girl in the Dollis Brook, 1959   182

Sources   189

Index   191

Preface & Acknowledgements

The title of this book was originally to be *Foul Deeds and Suspicious Deaths in the London Borough of Barnet*. However, I felt that this made it sound like an official publication, which would be entirely at variance with my intention. In any case, the inclusion of 'London Borough of Barnet' in the title would have been a bit of a misnomer: for example, the most recent murder covered in these pages occurred in July 1959, almost five years before the London Borough of Barnet came into being. Administratively speaking, the killing of Miriam von Young occurred in the Metropolitan Borough of Hendon. Nevertheless, the Borough of Barnet, as it currently stands, is the locale in which the tales of woe described in these pages take place. Therefore I will use the name 'Barnet' as a metonymic contraction to stand in for the collection of towns, villages or parishes that would one day be constituent parts of the administrative borough of that name. However, in describing each particular murder, I specify the town in which it took place, e.g. 'Hendon' or 'Finchley' etc. This is in order both to be consistent with events involving coroner's inquiries, newspaper reports and so forth, and to gain historical flavour. In accordance with my publisher's wishes, the cut-off date for this book is 1960. This was deemed desirable in order to spare the feelings of the families of victims. There were no murders in Barnet in 1960, although there was one in 1959, and so that is where the story ends. Murder is never funny, and writing this history has been a strain at times. However, I feel that, as well as providing a useful contribution to local studies, these retrieved fragments of regional memory – disasters and tragedies that extend like dark waves of recall far beyond the lives of both victim and persecutor – enable the reader to bear witness to the injustice of murder.

Special thanks are due to the London Borough of Barnet (LBB in picture credits) at their local studies library for their help and kindness and for permission to use a selection of images from their collection.

Introduction

Barnet is the third largest London borough. It comprises the old Middlesex metropolitan boroughs of Hendon, Finchley and Friern Barnet as well as the former Barnet and East Barnet Urban District Councils, in Hertfordshire. These previously distinct administrative areas had roots that can be traced farther back to various parishes and manorial tracts.

The London Borough of Barnet perhaps epitomises the idea of the 'suburban', where that word is taken to mean dull and lacking in drama, both of human life and of physical feature. Yet a little effort applied to defamiliarising the landscape, either by purposeful exploration or through the study of local history, throws the place into stark relief once again – if not for the first time. In order to 'frame' the zone within which the murders described in this book occurred I undertook a series of long walks crossing the borough in order to examine the site of each killing.

It quickly became apparent that Barnet was not the featureless zone I had presumed it to be. On the contrary – a quiet yet brooding power lurks in our hilly region of serried rooftops and arterial roads. A walk down the Hendon Way from my home in Child's Hill, in April 2007, revealed traces of the old Hendon Urban District Council sewage farm still visible in concrete culverts and the raised lines of a buried aqueduct at Brent Cross. Working up from there to Hendon, to Sunny Hill Park (noting along the way the old Hendon Corporation metals set into alleyways and road surfaces), I gazed over to the line of ridges running east to west along the northern rim of old Middlesex. I allowed my eyes to roll far off, across the landscape beyond Harrow-on-the-Hill, to Haste Hill at Ruislip and to windy Harefield on the western border of Middlesex. Next, after cutting through to Millfield Park in

Mill Hill via Arrandene Open Space, I looked west once more. From here the elongated ridge of Kingsbury Hill, Barn Hill and Harrow (elongated ridges from this perspective) looked like dreadnoughts in line abreast. And further beyond twinkled the lights of distant trunk roads and the tower blocks at Hounslow Heath.

That particular walk ended at Clay Lane, high up in the north of the Borough, on the South Hertfordshire tertiary escarpment. Here, in 1931, two tramps, Oliver Newman and William Shelley (known to their fellows as 'Tiggy' and 'Moosh' respectively) bludgeoned a fellow itinerant, 'Watford Pigsticker', to death, a crime for which they were hanged. This event, discovered during my researches for this book, challenged my notion of Barnet as a place with no history, no story to tell. Walking to where it happened provided me with a geographic framework within which to suspend the event and also illustrated graphically the broader sweep of regional history, the vast backdrop to these sad little tales.

In writing this book I decided that the linking of a killing to the borough could be done in several ways. Most obviously, the murder could take place in Barnet. Secondly, the victim or perpetrator could reside within the borough, yet have had their engagements with murder outside it. Finally, the killer or victim could have had a more tenuous connection with the borough, perhaps having grown up there or lived there some time prior to the event. I quickly discounted the third category as providing too slender a justification for the inclusion of any particular case. Of the second class, there are only three cases included here: the Edgware schoolgirl, Avril Ray Waters, thrown under a tube train at Tottenham Court Road tube station in 1939; Alfred Rouse's killing of an unknown person at Hardingstone in Northamptonshire in 1930; Ernest Walter Smee's murder of his common-law wife in Queensbury in 1937 – a crime widely reported as 'the Edgware Murder'.

There was another killing that occurred in such close proximity to the borough bounds that I felt tempted to try to sneak it in as 'my own'. This 'close run' occurred in February 1896. An old gentleman, Henry Smith, was murdered during

tion of Roque's map of Finchley, 1746. LBB

a botched burglary close to Coldfall Woods, at Muswell Hill Lodge in what is now Tetherdown Road. It was tempting to claim this case for my book but in the end this would have amounted to theft; the act occurred outside the borough by a hundred yards or so, and that is that.

I have not discussed the supposed murder of Nan Clark, although it is a vital part of the folklore of the borough. The lady in question gives her name to a lane running from Highwood, Mill Hill towards Moat End Farm. Nan Clark is described variously as having met her end through having her throat sliced, through being beheaded, or through being drowned in a pond as a wanton. However, there is no clear evidence who Nan Clark even was or what became of her, and unless her ghost, which is occasionally sighted walking the lane, decides one day to divulge the facts, we will probably never know. Nan Clark's Lane does however have a circumstantial connection with an actual verifiable murder, the shooting of John Child in 1941, so the residents of this pretty place needn't feel too left out.

I have rejected cases of death arising from the carrying out of illegal abortions though they often resulted initially in a charge of murder. There were a large number of such cases recorded in the local press, the account usually couched in language that was far from explicit. The inevitable outcome was a reduction to manslaughter. The occasional 'gas tragedy' involving lovers intent on mutual suicide, one of whom survived and was subsequently charged with murder, have been rejected, as have mercy killings.

I also decided to reject those cases of infanticide in which the unfortunate mother was the agent of the killing. Courts were usually inclined to be lenient in such situations and rightly so, in my opinion: these are domestic tragedies pure and simple, and have no place in this work. On the other hand, there are numerous instances in this book of the killer's being declared criminally insane and therefore technically not guilty

The view from Hadley across to the Arts' Depot, Finchley, 2008. Peter Simon

of murder; occasional findings of manslaughter also occur. These cases are undoubtedly examples of 'foul deeds' and therefore were considered suitable for inclusion.

The actual addresses where murders took place are not given in this book. Anybody intent on finding these out for 'psychogeographic' reasons, or out of plain morbid interest, can easily do this by looking up the facts in the local papers stored at The British Library newspaper collection at Colindale, north London, or at Barnet Borough's own local studies archive in Daws Lane.

My choice of cases may strike the reader as odd: the first part of the book is a selection of 'early' murders, drawn for the main part from the Middlesex court rolls. The first occurs in 1564, the most recent in 1684. These set the tempo for what follows, providing a sort of template for the later killings covered in the book's second part. Attempted murder followed by self-immolation; lethal assault with blunt instrument or with knife; the cold killing of the helpless or the frail: cases of this type were common back then and, sadly, continue to be so today.

More recent murders – from 1882 onwards – form the bulk of this book. This is partly because the records covering this period are both easier to access and far more detailed. A further reason is that I am more interested in tracing events which occurred on ground with which I am familiar. By 1900 much of the infrastructure of modern Barnet was already in place: the railways, for instance, already sliced bravely through the region on their various routes north. Given that my aim in writing was to evoke a dark and destabilising resonance – echoes of events murmuring below the streets, roads and parks which form the backdrop to our everyday – I decided to focus far more on elements recognizable to anybody who walks or drives through the borough today.

I felt tempted to write a long chapter on Finchley Common, that near-mythic presence in our regional recall. However, the idea of trotting out the usual stories of highwaymen, footpads and gibbets failed to grip me. The subject is well covered elsewhere and limitations of space rendered it necessary to pass on that one!

'Fans' of the darker side of local studies will be puzzled that I haven't written about the so-called 'East Finchley Baby Farm Murders', a notorious case that ended in the hanging of Amelia Sach and Annie Walters at Holloway in 1903. The reason is simple: I intend to produce a work dedicated solely to that case in the near future.

Most of the crimes described in these pages occurred within the jurisdiction of the Metropolitan Police's S Division, with its divisional station at Golders Green. As a result, the attentive reader may notice the recurring presence of certain key characters, particularly from among the police who investigated the killings. In general I have not remarked upon this, leaving it to the individual reader to track the career of any particular officer should he or she so wish. One major presence in this book that, I feel, does merit a comment is that of the Coroner for Central Middlesex, Dr George Cohen, who presided over most of the inquests included here.

We first meet George Alexander Cohen in 1911, during the events following the murder of Alice Isabel Linford by George Baron Pateman. Cohen assumed the role of district coroner on 4 November 1910, replacing Dr Francis Danford Thomas. Dr Danford Thomas had recently opened the inquest on remains found at Hilldrop Crescent, Camden, which were believed to be those of Mrs Crippin. The inquest was adjourned for a week, and during that time Dr Danford passed away.

As a result the inquiry had to be reopened and Dr Walter Schroder was appointed temporary acting coroner. Shortly afterwards Dr Cohen was voted in as district coroner, having resigned his position on the Middlesex County Council to stand as a candidate. He held his position for thirty-one years before dying at the Redhill Hospital, Edgware in 1941.

Part One: Early Cases

CHAPTER 1

From the Middlesex Court Rolls

c.1500–1700

During the reigns of Edward VI, Elizabeth I and Charles I.

A great gift was bestowed upon the regional historian when, in 1882, the Middlesex County Council ordered the collected Middlesex Sessions of Court to be removed from Westminster, where they had lain gathering dust, to a specially built 'Muniment Room' designed by the county architect at the Clerkenwell Sessions House. In the process, the multifarious documents – some dating back to William II – were cleaned of their dirt and mould before being catalogued by A T Watson, a restorer from the library at the British Museum. As a result of this endeavour, the collection was found to comprise 10,118 volumes and 4,916 rolls, or bundles of documents.

In 1884, the Middlesex Record Society sought and gained permission to publish a series of translations of sessions-rolls beginning with those dating from the time of Edward VI and running through to the end of James I's reign. The first volume in the series appeared in 1886, and it is from this that I will present a selection of brief accounts of murder.

The earliest document in the volume dates from 3 January 1549; the last from 4 February 1603, a few weeks before the death of Elizabeth I. Included in the collection are cases tried at the Quarter Sessions and the Old Bailey, as well as some civil matters. Reading these, one is thrust into the dark world of law and justice in Tudor Middlesex. The modern reader would most likely be horrified at the harshness of punishments meted out by the courts; for example, it was considered

Remains of the past: the Glebeland, Finchley, 2007. The author

perfectly reasonable in the reign of Elizabeth to whip a man and burn his ear 'through to the gristle' with a hot iron, to the compass of one inch, for no other crime than being a vagabond. The only hope such a man or woman had for avoiding this fate was if some person agreed to take him or her into service. Should the unfortunate relapse back into vagabondage, the punishment was then death on the gallows.

Little is known about the cases listed below, other than what the rolls inform us of. Some accounts consist of notification of the issuing of a true bill (an order issued by a magistrate authorising that the accused should answer to a given charge) and tell us nothing concerning whether the person in question was eventually found guilty or not. In presenting those entries relevant to Hendon and Finchley, I have hoped to give some idea of the temper of the times, and to illustrate that – just as today – these were places where murderous violence erupted periodically. I have allowed the entries to 'speak for themselves' for the most part, though, where appropriate, I have provided a comment or two.

21 AUGUST, 6 ELIZABETH (1564).- Coroner's Inquisition-post-mortem, taken at Hendon co. Midd. On view of the body of Hugh Lewys, there lying dead: with verdict that, at Hendon on the 15th inst. Ralph Houghton, late of Hendon yoman, assaulted the same Hugh Lewys and then and there murdered him by giving with a dagger a mortal wound in the left side, of which he died on the present 21st of August.

Houghton would seem to have been lucky, for the jury found him not guilty of murder. Sadly, however, they then found him guilty of the (then) lesser charge of homicide, and he was hanged anyway!

19 JUNE, 11 ELIZABETH (1569),- True Bill that at Fynchley co. Midd. On the said day Geoffrey Poole late of London gentleman assaulted Edward Welshe husbandman, and murdered him by giving him with a sword a mortal wound on the left side of his breast, of which wound he then and there died instantly.

Geoffrey Poole was recorded as still being at large the following April.

15 MAY, 41 ELIZABETH (1599).- True Bill that, at Fincheley co. Midd. On the said day, in a place of the said parish called Colefall, Freman Norton, alias Avery late of Fincheley aforesaid tayler assaulted Robert Haynes, being in God's and the Queen's peace, and with a handbill murdered the said Robert by giving him on the left part of his head a wound, of which he then and there died instantly. G.D.R., 41 Eliz.

The final item in this inventory occurs a few years later, during the reign of Charles I. Apparently, the half-century between this and the previous account had seen little or no softening in the punishments handed out by the courts:

5 FEBRUARY, 20 CHARLES I (1645).- A true bill was found against Edwin Seaman and Charles Walrond, both late of Finchley, Gentlemen, for assaulting Francis George at Finchley, when he was in God's and the King's peace, and that Edward Seaman then and there gave the said Francis George on his breast a mortal wound, of which he then and there died instantly.

Edward Seaman was sentenced to be hanged; Charles Walrond was found not guilty.

Murder is possibly a crime of sufficient gravity to justify capital punishment – or so many would argue. But who are the criminals, and whom the victims, in the numerous other cases listed in the rolls, of small-time thieves being hanged for petty pilfering? Witchcraft was also punishable by death. The next chapter contains a brief account of a woman being executed as a consequence of what may seem, to modern minds, as unsafe a conviction as it is possible to imagine.

CHAPTER 2

A Case of Witchcraft

1615

For practising witchcraft…so as to kill and murder…

Looking through the gaps between suburban houses, we often gain a glimpse of old oak or ash trees growing somewhere further off, in back gardens or on the Green Belt. In the winter the bare black boughs of the trees seem to writhe threateningly as they tower over the semi-detacheds like vast Kalis. These giants serve to remind us that, interpenetrating the electrically lit safety of our double-glazed homes and the ruthless quest for utility manifest in our concretised front gardens, there is an older world which will not go away, a realm whose concerns are not those of the human one.

Such, perhaps, was how witchcraft appeared to the seventeenth century mind. Even in as large a city as London there was a sense of the imminence of untamed forces. Everywhere lurked the danger of the supernatural and of entities that were beyond human control. There were also those strange men and women who were suspected of engaging with these beings rather than with the day-lit concerns of commerce and religion. As a result, both church and state colluded to rid society of these affronts to God's Law, to Man's world.

A great fear of witchcraft surfaced throughout Europe during the Renaissance, and in the period from roughly 1550 to 1700 a large number of supposedly scholarly books were published on the subject. Many of these works became accepted as authoritative by judges and lawyers, and none more so than James I's tract, *Demonology*, which brought royal sanction to bear on witch prosecutions. James' 1604 statute made hanging mandatory 'for a first offence of witchcraft' (one wonders what the sentence would be for a second offence). Though prosecutions frequently arose as a consequence of unexplained deaths being attributed to acts of witchcraft, the death sentence applied even if the offence did not amount to what was ostensibly murder. Nevertheless, the majority of witch trials arose as the result of injury for which there was no apparent explanation, other than the occult activities of someone who had acquired a sinister reputation, or whose behaviour or appearance was in some way unusual. While the total number of executions for witchcraft in England is now generally taken as being far lower than was thought at one point, this would be of scant comfort to those who suffered the torture and execution attendant upon being suspected and/or found guilty of practising 'the craft'.

The need to exact confessions from the accused was a vital component in securing convictions for witchcraft. The so-called 'swimming' of the accused – in which the poor unfortunate was thrown into a river or lake, their guilt or innocence defined respectively by whether they floated or drowned – is merely the best-known of the ordeals suffered in such cases. Frequent recourse to enforced isolation, whipping, starvation, burning and other tortures assured that the prosecution had a high probability of success when the case came to trial.

The Middlesex County Records contains accounts of two trials for witchcraft held in Finchley, one of which resulted in death for the accused, the other in acquittal. The trial described below took place with the full authority of law. Many today would see it as little more than legalised murder born of ignorance and prejudice:

> *17th January. 12th James I* [1615] *A true bill was found against Elizabeth Rutter, widow, for having practised at Fynchley certain wicked, detestable and devilish arts called inchauntmentes, charmes and sorceries, upon and against a certain Priscella Fielde, daughter of James Fielde, so that the said Priscella Fielde languished from the 17th January till the 18th of the same month, on which last named day she died of the said arts, being in this way murdered.*
> *Elizabeth Rutter was found guilty and sentenced to be hanged.*

The same file contains three further bills issued against Elizabeth Rutter:

1. *For practising witchcraft upon and against William Lyon, the son of John Lyon, on 1st November, 12 James I., so that he languished thereof from that day even to the date of the present inquisition, and still so languishes.*
2. *For practising witchcrafts on the 30th January, 12 James I., upon and against Frances Fielde, daughter of the above-mentioned James Fielde, so as to kill and murder her on the 31st day of the same month.*
3. *For practising the same hateful arts on 18th February, 12 James I., upon and against John Fielde, son of the same aforementioned James Fielde, so as to kill and murder him on the 1st March then next following.*

Elizabeth Rutter was found guilty and sentenced to be hanged.

The records are less than detailed as to the exact nature of the events surrounding the death of John Fielde etc. Whether Elizabeth Rutter actively injured the victims in some way, or was merely on the receiving end of an injustice, perhaps born of something as simple as neighbourly strife, we cannot say.

Another accusation of witchcraft is recorded in the following account, from several years later:

7th March. 16th James I. [1619] A true bill was found against Agnes Miller, Wife of Robert Miller, late of Fynchley, yeoman, for having practised certain devilish arts called inchantments, charms and sorceryes, upon and against Richard Harte, son of Solomon Harte, so that the said Richard Harte forthwith languished and continued to languish of the said arts until he died of them on the 14th day of the same month.

On her arraignment Agnes Miller put herself not guilty, and was acquitted.

Perhaps Agnes Miller was lucky – the years covered here were particularly bad ones for 'witches' – or possibly the acquittal is indicative of the King's growing scepticism regarding witchcraft following a series of injustices resulting from false testimony. Either way, we can see that early seventeenth century Finchley was not spared the beliefs and prejudices of its age.

The last execution for witchcraft in England took place at Exeter in 1684 and the death penalty for such was abolished by the Witchcraft Act of 1736.

CHAPTER 3

The Man who Murdered Himself

1684

He went down stairs and fetched a basin and a butcher's knife...

For many centuries, the Church considered the act of suicide to be a mortal sin and, as a result, those who died by their own hand were denied a Christian burial. By the tenth century, suicide was considered not just a sin but an actual crime. English common law distinguished a suicide, who was, by definition, of unsound mind, from a *felo-de-se* or 'felon against himself', who had decided to end it all, and thereby perpetrated an infamous crime.

Such a person forfeited his entire estate to the crown. Furthermore, his corpse was subjected to public indignities such as being dragged through the streets and hanged from the gallows, and was finally consigned to 'ignominious burial,' as the legal scholars put it—the favoured method was beneath a crossroads with a stake driven through the body. As time went on the punishments lessened, and by the seventeenth century a suicide merely forfeited his personal property; any real estate being passed on to his heirs. But the basic notion of suicide as a crime remained: ignominious burial wasn't abolished until 1823, nor property forfeiture till 1870, and the deed – whether successful or otherwise – remained a crime (albeit only a misdemeanour, and a rarely prosecuted one at that) until 1965. Logically this meant that all suicides were guilty of the unlawful killing of themselves and therefore, in effect, murderers.

The extract presented below was published originally in October 1684 as a folio newssheet, and was subsequently reprinted in full in *Finchley and Neighbourhood* by J R Biggers, in 1903. Following on from Mr Biggers, I reproduce the account in full: spellings are as in the original:

Strange and Bloody
N E W S
Of a most horrible
M U R D E R

Committed on the 26th instant October at
F I N C H L E Y
Near
Brown's Well
In
MIDDLESEX

In the parish of *Finchly* in the County of Middlesex, about six Miles from London, lived *Thomas Cover*, a young man, and a farmer, who falling in love with *Elizabeth Draper*, a Farmer's Daughter of the same parish, made his Court to her; who, though she was at first very coy, and slighted his affections (having choice of suitors, whom her beauty and virtuous education had attracted) yet at last, she resolved that *Thomas Cover* should be that happy man, who should carry the prize from all the rest of the Numerous Pretenders. Their Relations, who were mutually consulted, considering the equality of their fortunes, and the honest reputation they both lived in; thought it might prove a very agreeable Match, and as they had all along given them encouragement in their Amours, for now at last they contented to the finishing those Espousals which they hoped would make them both happy in each others Embraces.

The Ceremonious part of their Courtship being over, *Thomas Cover* asked her when they should be married, she answered she could not tell, but her Mother sitting by, told her it was her part to appoint the day, that now that everything was ready (for she had two New Gowns, a black one and a coloured, brought home by the Taylor two days before, and he, two Suits of Cloths) the sooner it was completed the better, for they had time little enough, to settle themselves in their New House, before Winter would come on.

Elizabeth her Daughter seemed to take little notice of her discourse: when her Sweet-Heart *Thomas* asked her when it should be, I can't tell said she, I am in no haste, and to tell you the truth, I think 'tis better as it is.

What, says *Thomas*, is your mind altered so Suddenly? No indeed, says she, I am resolved to the contrary.

Upon this *Thomas Cover* appeared very Melancholy, and went up to his Bed (his Lodging being in the same House) and after he had walked an hour or two in his Chamber, pondering upon the matter, he went down Stairs and fetched up a Bason of water and a great Butchers Knife they used to kill Hogs with; the Water as it is supposed, was to wash his hands after he had imbrued them in the Blood of his unkind and unconstant Mistriss whose death he was now resolved upon.

About twelve on Munday Night, the sixth of this Instant October, all the Family being in Bed and a sleep, he put off his Shooes, and with his Knife in his hand stole into her Chamber, which was hard by, and finding her fast asleep, put out the Candle which was there burning upon the occasion of a young Childs being sick, that lay with her, and afterwards going to the Bedside, feeling for her throat endeavoured to cut it; but having a Calico Hood on, which she usually lay in, ty'd with a Knot under her Chin, as he intended the Fatal Stroke, the Knot sav'd it from her flesh, though on one side there was a great gash, but which is hop'd it will not be Mortal.

At this she awaked and cryed out, when *Thomas Cover* went down Stairs and out of the House into an adjacent Close and immediately with the same Knife cut his own throat, from Ear to Ear of which he presently died, and was the next Morning found there, and the Knife by him.

Mr. Harris the Coroner, who lives at Clarken well being acquainted with it Summoned a Jury of the Neighbours who lived at *Finchly*, who upon the plainness of the Circumstances, brought him Guilty of his own Murder.

Part Two: Modern Times

CHAPTER 4

Death in Coppett's Wood

1884

I arrest you for the murder of your mate Clarke in Finchley Wood.

The period following from the Enclosure Act of 1811 saw great changes to the landscape of Finchley. The old Finchley Common – notorious for highwaymen and footpads – was parcelled out as fields for local landowners; and housing sprang up along the major roads linking formerly distant hamlets. When, a few years later, the arrival of the railways brought successful businessmen to the area seeking peace and quiet away from the city, Finchley began to be associated with affluence. Unfortunately for the residents of Finchley – both old and new – the combination of railways and these emergent pockets of wealth also brought crime in their wake.

Burglary is a constant in the world of crime, yet the mid-to late-nineteenth century witnessed an increase, both in the frequency of this offence and in sophistication of technique. It was not uncommon for teams of specialists in the art to travel out from London to the new suburbs, where rich pickings could be stolen from the fine houses and villas belonging to a more successful stratum of society.

Yet not all was enclosure and development: areas of woodland survived – and continue to do so into the present day – and one of these, Coppett's Wood, was scene for a killing that ranks along with the best that the old tales of Finchley Common have to offer.

It was the evening of Saturday, 4 March 1884. Walter Brinkley and his uncle, James Brinkley, both members of a gypsy camp located at Irish Corner (close by where Coppett's Road joins the North Circular Road today), were wandering about in the woods looking for a lost pony, when they came upon a black felt hat lying on the ground. A few yards further on, they stumbled across the body of a man lying in the undergrowth. Drawing close, the Brinkleys noticed that the man's throat had been severely wounded. They ran off to the local smallpox hospital and related what they'd seen to the porter, who returned with them to the site. They were shortly joined by PC Plowman, 298 Y Division, and Dr Langford, a local GP. A brief inspection assured the policeman that this was, indeed, a dead man, his right hand placed across his breast and his clothes heavily bloodstained. The cadaver was removed to a shed behind the *Bald Faced Stag* public house in East End (present day East Finchley).

Here Dr Langford subjected the body to a post-mortem examination, which revealed that the victim had been dead for several hours. The man's throat bore extensive injuries, and his body had also been subjected to repeated assault with a sharp instrument. Dr Langford was of the opinion that the wounds could not have been self-inflicted and that they pointed to a severe struggle having occurred. A police murder inquiry was set up, headed by Inspector Charles Dodd, chief of the CID at Y Division. Dodd immediately organised a search for the murder weapon in the area where the body had been found.

In the company of his assistant, Sergeant Lucas, Dodd searched Coppett's Wood closely. Sifting through the undergrowth, they presently came upon a hamper containing silver and plated spoons and, near to where the body had lain, were found four empty wine bottles.

This provided Dodd with his first lead, as the spoons were quickly linked to a burglary that had taken place on the previous Friday at St Alban's Villa, Friern Barnet, the home of a Mr Hill. It was possible that further items from the haul would eventually appear, and hopefully lead the police to the murderer.

The newspapers of the day expressed considerable excitement at the discovery of the body, *The Times* describing the unfolding drama on a day-by-day basis. Public interest was intensified by the fact that nobody seemed able to identify who the victim had been. *The Times* issued a police photograph and description of the man found, hoping this would help to identify him. He was described thus:

> *Aged between 25 or 30, height 5 ft. 9in., complexion fair, hair very light brown, no whiskers, but a few hairs on upper lip, eyes light gray, eyebrows light, thick lips, large nose, high cheek-bones, full neck, well built but slightly, very long hands and fingers; dress black, diagonal coat, part of a black cloth vest, (velvet collar, Vandyke velvet lacings), black tweed trousers, white plaid scarf.*

The publicity prompted various persons to come forward, claiming to have identified the deceased. One of these in particular, Samuel Outing, a shoemaker from Highgate, thought he recognized the body as that of Peter Butler, a gypsy from Brentwood.

A gang of workmen reported having heard loud cries of 'murder' from the direction of the woods as they'd walked along Colney Hatch Lane on the day of the killing, but thinking that the cries were those of somebody exercising their voice they had taken no notice.

The inquest was held on 8 March at the *Bald Faced Stag*. Dr Danford Thomas presided, and evidence was heard from the Brinkleys, the police, and other witnesses. Samuel Outing once more swore to the identity of the deceased as being that of the gypsy Peter Butler. Walter Brinkley (who was also a gypsy and therefore might have been expected to know) on the other hand claimed that the murder victim was completely unknown to him and on this point his uncle agreed. PC Plowman described the position and state of the body. Dr Langford presented his conclusions arising from the post-mortem examination and reiterated that the injuries to the body were the result of a violent struggle. The evidence having been heard, the coroner instructed the jury as to the impossibility at arriving at any conclusion other than that the deceased had been murdered. The jury concurred, returning a verdict of wilful murder against some person or persons unknown.

Shortly afterwards, the police declared that their inquiries had revealed that Peter Butler was alive and well. The police then put up a reward of £100 and a free pardon to any accomplice who forwarded information as to the identity of the murderer. At the same time an announcement was placed in *The Times* enjoining the 'utmost vigilance upon all pawnbrokers and second-hand dealers to keep an eye out for goods as yet unrecovered from the burglary'. These included a distinctive midshipman's telescope covered in black morocco, a silver fruit knife with a mother-of-pearl handle and a family volume of Shakespeare in a brown binding.

Perhaps it was anguish at the loss of a loved one rather than the offer of financial reward that prompted Emily Matthews, an unmarried woman living in The Borough, south London, to contact the police with her concerns. Either way, she made contact with the forces of law and order and was able to identify the clothes found on the body as having belonged to Enoch Clarke, her lover. She described how she had been in lodgings with Clarke and another man, John Baker, twenty-two, at a house in Mint Street, Borough. She had last seen Clarke on 2 March, when he and Baker had left together 'on some business'. The following morning at about 11am Baker had returned alone to the lodging house. Upon being asked where Clarke was, Baker answered that he would turn up in a few minutes, but when he did not turn up Emily Matthews again asked about Clarke. Baker said he would go and find him, and left the house. He returned in the evening with a quantity of items in a hamper. These included silver-plated nutcrackers and other obvious booty from a robbery. She noted on that occasion that Baker's coat was spotted with blood. He claimed that this was a consequence of having knocked a policeman senseless with a bottle of wine in order to get away. Baker then claimed that Clarke had been caught and was in police custody. Matthews later pawned some tablecloths and a pair of child's boots at Baker's request.

Statements were duly taken from Matthews, and the police closed in on their man. A Detective Harvey met Baker coming from a public house in King William Street in the City, took hold of him and said, 'I arrest you for the murder of your mate Clarke in Finchley Wood.' Baker answered, 'That's what you say, but that has got to be proved.' He was handcuffed, and led across London Bridge. During the arrest a crowd had gathered, and some small boys began to hurl abuse at the prisoner. Baker threatened them and refused to walk any further, a cab then being procured to convey him into custody. Here Baker confessed to the burglary but denied any knowledge of the murder.

John Baker appeared at the Highgate Petty Sessions before Mr W P Bodkin on 18 March. He was charged with 'burglarously entering St Alban's Villa' on 2 March, and with having committed 'the wiful murder of Enoch Clarke in Cobbitts Wood, Finchley, on the same night'.

Emily Matthews' statement was read out to the court, further evidence being provided by Chief Inspector Dodd. Baker pleaded guilty to burglary but denied having murdered his accomplice. He was duly remanded in custody.

Matthews made a further statement in which she described how Clarke and Baker had frequently come to blows over her affections, the former accusing his friend of having an affair with Matthews during periods he had spent away from Mint Street. This was raised at Baker's next appearance at Highgate on 23 March. Mr Pollard, the counsel for the prosecution, indicated to the court that he had been instructed by the Director of Public Prosecutions to seek the prosecution of the accused for the crime of murder. He stressed that the burglary, while a lesser offence, had preceded and led directly to the more serious offence, it therefore being necessary to present evidence of Baker's involvement in the earlier crime. Once more Baker was remanded in custody, to reappear before the court on 29 March.

There were suggestions within the police force that Baker and Clarke were members of the so-called 'Black Gang', a group of violent robbers living in The Borough. This resulted in what, today, we would call a leak to the press. The *Penny Illustrated* gave a brief account of the court proceedings under a banner proclaiming Baker's membership of the gang, yet despite such presumption on the part of the publishers no connection between Baker and the gang was ever proved.

In the meantime, a meerschaum pipe originating from St Alban's Villa had turned up at a pawnbroker's in Blackfriars Road. This was traced back to Frederick Checkley, a labourer from Mint Street. A statement was duly taken in which Checkley said that the pipe had been handed to him by Baker some days before the arrest. He also recalled seeing blood spots on Baker's boots and trousers at the time.

Baker's next court appearance led to his being remanded in custody yet again. To date he had not had any representation in court and, with the police evidence nearly complete, was due to appear for committal proceedings prior to trial by jury. It was deemed necessary that he have someone to speak for him in court, so at his final appearance at Highgate he was represented by a Mr Poncione, who advocated fiercely for his client throughout. It did no good, however, and Baker was committed for trial at the Old Bailey on the charge of murder.

The trial opened on 6 May before Mr Justice Hawkins, and lasted three days. The evidence against Baker was so strong that his defence played upon the uncertainty as to motive and this saved Baker from a death by hanging. The fact that Baker and Clarke had been known to come to blows over Emily Matthews on previous occasions was used to great effect, it being argued that Baker had not intended to kill his companion. Clarke's death was an accidental outcome of what was nothing more than a physical fight between the two men.

On the other hand, it was pointed out by the prosecution that Clarke was a big man; that he had been a grenadier guardsman; and that he had been pierced nineteen times by a stabbing instrument. Yet *Baker* bore no wounds whatsoever. The prosecution argued that this indicated that Baker took

Clarke at a disadvantage, which pointed to clear and cold-blooded murder.

Surprisingly, perhaps, the jury found Baker guilty, not of murder but of manslaughter and he was thus spared the noose. And despite receiving a sentence of penal servitude for life, Baker left the dock smiling: in the harsh criminal world of The Borough this would undoubtedly have counted as a 'result'.

The Times commented on the case at length. Drawing its imagery from Charles Dickens' *Oliver Twist,* the editorial pointed out that there were still large areas of the metropolis inhabited by real life Fagins and Artful Dodgers. Emily Matthews was clearly the 'Nancy' of the piece in all save Nancy's final fate. *The Times* then sought to abstract a moral from the affair, presenting this in somewhat lurid terms:

Those who live among the pleasant scenes of Finchley, whose villas nestle among the woods thereabouts, may begin to remember that the most delightful coppices, like the most luxuriant creepers, serve, after all, to harbour vermin.

CHAPTER 5

Who Killed Lydia Hill?

1895

*That the poor fellow who is at present charged with the
crime is guilty of such a combination of brutal villainy
it is difficult to believe.*

East Barnet is part of that 'other' London Borough of Barnet, lying in the valley of Pymme's Brook to the east of the old Great North Road. Whereas Hendon and Finchley were once located in Middlesex, East Barnet remains a part of Hertfordshire, a county with its own customs and attitudes. Perhaps because of this there is still something about the place that renders it remote from the racy cosmopolitanism of North Finchley or Golders Green. When the Great Northern Railway arrived in the area in the late-1860s, creating the suburb of New Barnet to the northwest, East Barnet began to grow. However, at the time described here there was still a distinctly rural air to the place. The 1896 Ordnance Survey map shows the land between the *Prince of Wales* public house at the foot of Cat Hill and the railway bridge on Long Street (today's Longmore Avenue) to have been empty of housing. There were, in those days, a number of fields intersected by streams where, today, Berkeley Crescent and Trevor Close stand; it was in one of these, a field close to Lancaster Road, that the victim of a particularly horrible murder was discovered.

It was the spring of 1895 and Lydia Hill was fast approaching her eighth birthday. She lived with her family in Rose Cottages at the south end of Lancaster Road, one of a series of streets commemorating the 1471 Battle of Barnet in the Wars of the Roses. Lydia was a perfectly normal little girl

The railway bridge at Longmore Avenue (Long Street), 2008. Peter Simon

who could no doubt be somewhat self-willed and given to occasional naughty behaviour. Her father, William, was a coal merchant who had moved into the area from north Hertfordshire several years previously.

On the evening of Wednesday, 17 April Lydia asked her father if she could go outside to play with a friend. Both Mr and Mrs Hill were suffering badly form head colds, so their resolve to resist the child's entreaties was perhaps fatally weakened. Lydia ran off to play with her friends, and although she had not yet returned by tea-time, her parents were not unduly concerned. Later, they sent her brothers and sisters out to search for her in the failing light. No trace of Lydia could be found, despite inquiries being made at her friends' homes, and concern began to grow for her safety. Accordingly, a message was passed on to the police at New Barnet informing them of Lydia's disappearance. Despite this, it was a member of the public who eventually discovered the child's awful fate.

At about 9.20 the next morning William Davidson, a neighbour of the Hills', entered Nicholls' Field, just behind his house, in order to tend a small vegetable plot he kept there. To his horror he stumbled across the body of a child lying on her back in the grass, and instantly recognised it as that of Lydia. The girl had a skipping rope in one hand and her face was quite black. At that moment Davidson saw a local policeman, Sergeant George Jewell, who was about to enter the Hills' front gate, presumably to make inquiries about the missing girl. Davidson called the policeman over, his shout bringing the unfortunate Mr Hill to his door. Mr Hill and Sergeant Jewell rushed over to see what Davidson had found, and, upon seeing his daughter dead in the grass, Mr Hill buried his face in his hands and wept with grief.

While William Davidson escorted Mr Hill back to Lancaster Road, Sergeant Jewell sent a boy off to inform the local GP, Dr Roughton, and to alert the police station at New Barnet. He then examined the body more closely, noting that Lydia Hill's arms were outstretched and that the right knee was bent, and placed slightly under the left leg. Her clothes were in a state of disarray and the underclothes had clearly been tampered with. Lying in the grass close by was a shiny new penny.

Dr Roughton arrived soon after and promptly declared Lydia Hill dead, the body being removed to the *Warwick Tavern* to await inquest. Sergeant Jewell was then joined by Detective Inspectors Waddell and Dowty from Whetstone Police Station. Scotland Yard was informed of the murder and Superintendent Wren and Inspector White of the CID travelled up to New Barnet by train to supervise the inquiry.

Later that day Dr Roughton performed an autopsy on the dead girl. Notes taken at the time of her discovery suggested that Lydia had been dead nine or ten hours. The child had clearly been sexually violated some time before her death. Dr Roughton concluded that death had been due to strangulation.

In the meantime, all sorts of ugly rumours began to surface in the understandably fraught atmosphere of East Barnet. Thomas Osborn, a local man, aged thirty-four, who was generally considered to be a bit of an eccentric and drunk, had been seen in the area the previous evening. Worse, a local girl, Ada Baker, claimed to have actually seen Lydia Hill walking down Long Street with Osborn late in the day. Another girl, Ettie Julian, told the investigating officers that she'd seen Osborn earlier that evening in Lancaster Road. She had been sent out on an errand in the course of which Osborn had approached her and said, 'I'll have you when you come back.' Later, on her return – it was now quite dark – a lamp had been shone in her face by a man in a hedge. Ettie Julian heard a voice she thought was Osborn's say, 'Come along with me, my duckie,' and she had fled home in terror. The police were understandably concerned by this information, and Osborn was promptly arrested at his home, a tumbledown cottage close to the *Three Cups of Coffee* inn in Whetstone, and taken into custody for questioning by the police. Here he was asked to account for his movements on the night in question. While admitting to having been in the vicinity of Long Street, Osborn denied all knowledge of the murder. Upon being charged he was relieved of his clothes which were sent off to St Mary's Hospital for forensic analysis.

The following day he made a short appearance at Barnet Magistrates' Court, before H R Trotter, where he was formally charged with feloniously causing the death of Lydia Hill. He was further charged with the rape of the child. An ill-looking William Hill identified the murder victim and recounted the events of the previous Wednesday and Thursday. Sergeant Jewell then gave evidence regarding the discovery of the body, as did William Davidson. Dr Roughton informed the court of the result of the post-mortem. Both Ada Baker and Ettie Julian gave evidence linking Osborn to the crime.

Mr Trotter asked Osborn if he had any questions to put to the witnesses, to which Osborn replied, 'This is all strange news to me.' He was remanded in custody to Brixton Prison for the weekend.

The following Monday Osborn once again appeared at Barnet Magistrates' Court for the express purpose of being re-remanded prior to attending the opening of the coroner's inquest. This was a mere formality designed to assure that he could be effectively constrained by officers while in attendance.

The inquest was held in two parts, separated by a week's adjournment, at the *Warwick Tavern*, New Barnet. Presiding was R W Brabant, deputy coroner for the Liberty of St Albans. Osborn was present at both hearings. The police were once again represented by Inspectors Waddell and Dowty. Osborn was represented by Mr Edward Sweeting, a local solicitor.

The first hearing was taken up with the results of the post-mortem and testimony from Mr Hill, Sergeant Jewell and Mr Davidson. The inquest was then adjourned until 3 May. In the meantime the intrepid Sergeant Jewell had made further attempts to positively link Osborn to the scene of crime. He revisited Osborn's tumbledown cottage in order to see if grass seeds originating from Nicholls' Field could be found on the premises. However, contrary to expectation no such seeds were found and this seriously weakened the Crown's case as Osborn had been arrested at the cottage and reason suggested that had he been in Nicholls' Field on the night of the murder some seeds would have been carried with him in his clothing.

Lydia Hill's funeral took place at the Great Northern Cemetery, Brunswick Park Road, on Tuesday, 23 April. Prior to the internment a funeral service was held at the Wesleyan Chapel, New Barnet, by the pastor, the Reverend J Willis Britton. Both Lydia Hill's parents were members of the chapel and the girl had belonged to the Sunday school held there. A large number of people – including several uniformed police officers – attended both the service and the funeral.

When the inquest resumed the coroner informed the jury that the Crown had urged him not to finish the inquest that day as further evidence was still pending. In particular, Osborn's clothing had been subjected to microscopic analysis and there were hopes that this would provide conclusive evidence. The foreman of the jury, a Mr Baldwin, pointed out that they were there to inquire into the death of the child, and not as to who committed the murder; the jury were in just as good a position now as they would be when the evidence arrived. Mr Sweeting then took the opportunity to remonstrate with the coroner, pointing out that the delay in delivering the result of the analysis of the clothes was unacceptable – after all, the garments had merely to be placed under a microscope. In the meantime, his client had been in custody for nearly two weeks.

Dr Roughton gave evidence that he had analysed a handkerchief found on the prisoner at the time of his arrest, and that it was stained with blood.

The jury, after a short retirement, returned a verdict of wilful murder against some person unknown. Before the jury retired, Mr Sweeting said that if the jury came to such a decision he would like them to add a rider stating that, in their opinion, Osborn did not commit the murder. The coroner said that this could not be done. Nevertheless, the jury's decision may well have been an additional factor in the events which now followed.

The strong feeling aroused in the region by so terrible a murder caused the police to show a heavy presence at all of Osborn's subsequent appearances lest mob-rule should erupt. Yet, contrary to all expectation there emerged a strong groundswell of sentiment in favour of the accused. A letter, published in the *Barnet Press* on 4 May, gives voice to this by reminding the reader that, even in the present case, the law should be allowed its due process. After acknowledging the gravity of the offence, the writer goes on to say:

But the matter is still sub-judice and more of the grim details of this heinous act may possibly be made known. That the poor fellow who is at present charged with the crime is guilty of such a combination of brutal villainy, it is difficult to believe, and certainly on the present evidence.

After two further appearances at court Osborn appeared at the Barnet Petty Sessions for the final time on Monday, 14 May. Mr Colbeck appeared for the Crown, and Mr Sweeting once again represented the prisoner.

Mr Colbeck opened by stating that he had no intention of recounting the details of the offence as these were already well known both to the bench and, indeed, to the general public. The question with which he had to deal was as to whether there was any evidence before the court with a reasonable chance of bringing the charge home to the prisoner. The fact that Lydia Hill had been both outraged and murdered was indisputable. Certain information had then been placed in the hands of the police and this had resulted in Osborn's arrest. Mr Colbeck explained that the information given had been passed on to the Director of Public Prosecutions who had concluded that there was insufficient evidence to convict the prisoner. While both Lydia Hill and Osborn had been seen in Long Street on the night of the murder, they had not been seen together. What was made of the girl, Ada Baker's claim that she had seen them together has not been recorded, but was presumably discounted. The simple fact of their both being in the area that night was not sufficient to enable him to ask the court to commit the prisoner for trial. Further, the microscopic analysis had proved to be inconclusive.

Mr Sweeting followed up Colbeck's remarks with a reminder that he had asked the court for bail at each of the previous appearances and that Osborn had now been in custody for thirty days.

The chairman said he entirely concurred in the remarks made by the counsel for the Crown, and expressed regret that the prisoner should have been held for so long. Osborn was then released from custody to great cheers from his supporters, friends and family, who had crowded the public gallery.

On leaving the court Osborn was promptly surrounded by well-wishers and subjected to numerous slaps on the back. Amply supplied with both chewing tobacco and a lit pipe filled with Short Coloured Cutty, Osborn was led off, shrouded by a cloud of fragrant smoke, towards the top-end of Barnet. One imagines that the attractions of the *Red Lion* followed soon after. The police immediately reopened the murder case, but who it was that killed Lydia Hill has never been discovered.

CHAPTER 6

The College Farm Murder

1898

It was a very large bullet for a revolver.

un crime was no latecomer to Barnet. The next case occurred over a century ago, but perhaps the circumstances are readily recognisable to the modern sensibility.

College Farm is one of those surviving pockets of once-rural Middlesex that remain popular with conservationists, animal lovers and children. The sight of cows grazing in lush meadows, of the pretty poplar-lined cobblestone path leading up between fields to the old dairy house: who has not gazed out in wonder at this remarkable place from the window of their car or bus? And all within sight of the busy road junction where the A406 North Circular crosses the Finchley Road!

College Farm – the Express Dairy's 'model farm' – was opened in 1883. At that time the area was a quiet way-stage on the route between the hamlets of Golders Green and Finchley Church End, where trains could be picked up for London and a market provided goods for the locals. Apart from the farm there was a cluster of houses along Regent's Park Road, but otherwise the area was far quieter than it is today.

In 1897, Thomas Webb, a Wiltshire man, arrived at the farm together with his wife, Sophie. The couple, who had been married for two years, moved into the farm building, living above the entrance in its north-east corner. Webb was a quiet, hard-working, and sensible man. He was head cowman, and good at his job. And although he was hardly able to write, he did read well. Yet this otherwise down-to-earth man was haunted by a presentiment. Reading in the newspapers in

College Farm c.1900. LBB

January 1898 of the trial of Richard Price for the shooting of the Shakespearean actor William Terriss outside the Adelphi Theatre, Webb exclaimed to his wife that he fancied *he* would die by the bullet. However, the presentiment was not so strong, or Webb so irrational, as to allow his conduct to be thus directed.

It was on the night of Saturday, 29 January that the events here described occurred. The other farm workers were away, either in town for a drink or out of the area, visiting family. At about eight o'clock Webb turned to his wife and told her he was off to check over the farm, after which he intended to walk to Finchley to buy provisions. He picked up his stick and a bag and set off, walking down the small drive connecting the farm to Regent's Park Road. Being winter it was pitch black at this hour but Sophie, his wife, wasn't too worried. Webb had told her he'd be back at about 9.00 pm. Yet within minutes of leaving her, Thomas Webb returned, falling through the farmhouse door and crying 'Sophia', Sophia'. Rushing to her husband, Sophie Webb heard him exclaim, 'I am shot,' as he

A farm worker at College Farm, c.1895. LBB

fell to the ground. Blood was spurting from the side of his neck, and he attempted to staunch this with his hand. Mrs Webb set off immediately for help, to 'Westward,' a large house in Regent's Park Road where an acquaintance, Mrs Pate, lived. Robert Mackenzie, a local barrister, joined the two women, and together they hurried to the farmhouse where they found the unfortunate Mr Webb in a state of collapse. The poor man was carried up to his bedroom and Drs Harper and Godfrey, from Finchley, were soon in attendance. However, they arrived too late and Dr Harper's skills were required to extend no further than declaring Mr Webb dead.

The police arrived shortly after this in the form of Inspector Scrase and Superintendent Dodd, who had been on duty at Finchley. They were later joined by Inspector Rowan, CID, and other detectives from Scotland Yard, these having been telegraphed for.

After a brief examination, Dr Harper expressed the opinion that Webb had been shot, and that a bullet had entered the left side of the neck, severing the jugular before lodging in the opposite side. He dismissed the idea of suicide. The police immediately set off to scour the area and find the assailant but were unsuccessful. It was a dark night and, as mentioned, College Farm was far more remote in those days. Footpaths led from the farm towards Finchley, Golders Green and Hendon, and the killer could have taken any of these in his escape.

A quantity of blood was found just outside the door to the farmhouse, close to the entrance to the rick-yard, this leading the police to believe that the latter was where the assassin had hidden prior to the shooting.

A North Finchley laundryman, Henry Morris, gave the police some potentially useful information. He had been delivering some laundry to Braeside, a house on Regent's Park Road on the night in question. Mr Morris had heard the sound of shots and, at about the same time, he'd seen a flickering light between the farm and the main road, and saw a man lighting a lamp on a bicycle. The man then mounted the bike and rode off towards London. Morris had business at Swiss Cottage and overtook the cyclist just by Finchley Road station. The light being good at this spot, Morris was able to note details of the man's features. He was about thirty-two years of age, and 5' 9" in height. His hair and moustache were fair.

The inquest on Thomas Webb was held at 10 o'clock that Thursday in the billiard room at the *Orange Tree* public house in Colney Hatch, before Dr G Danford Thomas, coroner for Central Middlesex. It was held outside the parish of Finchley in order to discourage unnecessary crowds from attending. Inspector Moore and Detective-Inspectors McCarthy and Rowan attended as representatives for Scotland Yard. The jury was formed of residents from Finchley and was headed by Mr E Southwell.

Sophie Webb was the first witness. She told the assembly her husband was on good terms with everybody. As she described the moment when her husband was shot she broke down and cried. Her husband did not manage to tell her who'd shot him. She described Webb's presentiment regarding the death of Terriss to the inquest. The news of the actor's death had helped him to tell his wife of his fears. According to Sophie Webb her husband had left off reading the news on the murder and said 'I never told you, but I have a strong presentiment...someone will shoot me.' She'd then asked him if anyone held a grudge against him, to which he'd replied that he didn't think so. Concerns were shown about the movements of the other farm workers that night, but Mrs Webb was able to assure the inquest that they had all been away.

Thomas Webb was buried at St Marylebone cemetery, on East End Road, a week after his murder. Perhaps out of respect for the widow far fewer people lined the route from College Farm to the burial place than might have been anticipated. The mourners included, besides Mrs Webb, G Titus Barham, managing director of Express Dairies, and several farm hands. Both the dairy company and Webb's immediate colleagues from the farm provided floral tributes.

Police inquiries continued. They carried out a rudimentary form of forensic ballistics, discharging a revolver, possibly similar to the one used in the shooting at a target, in order to determine the penetrative force of the bullet over varying distances. The results were inconclusive in so far as it got them no closer to discovering precisely where the killer had been located. However, they were able to assess the distance between the gun and Webb as being considerably more than a few feet.

A theory gained ground that Webb had died as a result of a spent bullet accidentally finding its way to him. This idea was discarded, however, when a close examination of the bullet's route through his body indicated that it had travelled upwards, whereas a spent bullet would be expected to gravitate earthwards. An examination of the farm between the buildings and Regent's Park Road revealed blood spots by a small bridge crossing a ditch close to the main road. A sparse thicket lined either side of the drive at this point and the police therefore considered the possibility that Webb's assailant may have hidden there, his crouching position presumably explaining the upward trajectory of the bullet. This would also explain the number of people claiming to have heard the shots from Regent's Park Road whilst no firing was heard at the farm.

But all this remained conjecture in the absence of an actual suspect, and progress in this area got nowhere. The *Hendon and Finchley Times* reported on the week of the funeral that 'something of a startling nature will be forthcoming at the adjourned inquest', though any reader who hoped this would involve an exposé of the identity of the villain was to be sorely disappointed.

The inquest was resumed two weeks later, Webb's widow once more weeping bitterly when the coroner read over the evidence that had been presented at the previous sitting. More witnesses were called to present evidence. The barrister, Robert Mackenzie, stated that he'd sometimes heard gun shots coming from the neighbourhood of the farm prior to the day of the shooting. He was positive that he'd heard two gun shots at about eight o'clock on the night of the deceased's death. There had been an interval of about four seconds between the reports. Dr Harper gave evidence that the wound was certainly not self-inflicted, his argument being that the bullet would have passed straight *through* the throat at such a short range.

The police brought in a gunsmith, Edwin John Churchill, who ran a workshop near the Strand, to present evidence on the type of gun used. (His nephew, Robert Churchill, was later to have a virtual monopoly over forensic ballistics carried out on behalf of the Metropolitan Police). Churchill was of the opinion that the bullet found embedded in Webb's neck was of foreign make. The fact the bullet had failed to penetrate his neck indicated that it had been fired from a distance in excess of 200 yards and had therefore been spent. This led Churchill to conclude that it was a chance shot fired by some reckless person. In the absence of more conclusive evidence the jury returned a verdict that the 'deceased had succumbed to the effects of a bullet wound fired by someone at present unknown, and with what intention there was no evidence to show'.

It is worth mentioning here that shortly before the Webb shooting a robbery involving a firearm had taken place in Bishop's Avenue, in those days a quiet backwater, a far cry from its modern incarnation as millionaire's row. A Mrs M Mathieson of East Finchley had been held up and robbed by a man 'of Herculean proportions' who had discharged the gun in her direction. Unfortunately, Mrs Mathieson had not been able to describe her assailant. It is interesting to note that although the robbery took place a mere seven days before the murder of Webb, the police, as far as can be discerned, failed to link the two offences.

Rumours surfaced in 1903 that a confession to the shooting was on the cards, the *Barnet Times* even reporting this; however, nothing came of it and, to date, we are no closer to knowing who shot Thomas Webb than in 1898.

CHAPTER 7

The Girl in the Silkstream

1909

I took a little girl from a field near Roundwood Park…
into a field behind the 'Stag'…

The electric tram arrived in Middlesex in the early part of the 1900s, following the building of a network of 'light railway lines' by the County Council. One of the new tram services ran up the Edgware Road from the *Spotted Dog* public house at Willesden, through West Hendon, to the village of Edgware. At first, this service had no substantial impact on housing or population; the land either side of what is known today as Burnt Oak Broadway was still mainly rural in the decades preceding the Great War. Buildings along that part of the road were restricted to the Hendon Union Workhouse and some scattered villas and farms. There was also a public house, The *Bald Faced Stag* (not to be confused with the pub of the same name at East Finchley). It was behind this place of refreshment, in a field running down to the Silkstream Brook that police officers came in the small hours of 18 June 1909. Carrying lanterns, and wrapped against the early morning chill, the officers were looking for a murdered child, following a startling confession made by a man initially arrested as a suspected burglar.

The man whose statement brought the police to this secluded spot was Frederick Burgess, twenty, a labourer living in Prospect Road, Child's Hill. Burgess had been picked up in Melrose Avenue, Cricklewood (a street which would gain notoriety years later for its association with the serial killer Denis Andrew Nilsen) by PC Battershill, of X Division, for

Silksteam Park – the site of the murder, 2007. The author

'loitering with intent to commit a felony' at 1.05 that morning. He was taken to Willesden Green Police Station and searched. Burgess was known to the police and had served time in Dartmoor Prison several years before. The suspicion was that Burgess had been preparing to burgle a house – not such an uncommon event. The routine police inquiry suddenly changed, however, when Burgess confessed to having picked up a small girl and murdering her a few days before. He claimed he had thrown her body in a brook, the name of which he did not know, but from a description he gave to the police it became clear he meant the Silkstream, near Edgware.

After gleaning more information from the suspect – including a description of a tram journey taken by Burgess and the girl, Detective Inspector Pike, Inspector Perry and Detective Sergeant Triton motored out to the stream close to the *Bald Faced Stag.* Dr Whitehall Cooke, the police divisional surgeon for X Division, accompanied them. Approaching the brook they found bloodstains on the grass, which appeared to confirm Burgess' statement, and then Inspector Perry waded

High Road at Edgware, c 1910. LBB

into the water. Almost at once he found the body of a little girl. After hauling the sad remains onto the bank of the brook they positioned their lamps for a closer inspection. This revealed five puncture wounds in the throat of the victim along with numerous other injuries elsewhere. The body was taken by ambulance to the mortuary at the new Hendon Town Hall, and placed into the care of PC Harwood, the coroner's officer.

It is probable that the police already suspected who the child was: a five-year-old girl, Annie Lydia Fletcher, had been reported missing from her home in Balmoral Road, Harlesden the previous Tuesday, 15 June. The girl lived there with her father, Walter John Fletcher, together with Mrs Brown, his common-law wife and her boy Sam. Annie went to Pound Lane School, and had been on her way there when she disappeared 'behind a hedge,' as Sam told the police. From all accounts Annie was a pretty little thing, with fair hair and bright blue eyes.

It was assumed that her intention had been to play truant and that Burgess had picked her up shortly afterwards. The unfortunate father was promptly summoned to the Hendon mortuary where he identified the body as that of his little child. He also recognised a white straw hat, on which was written 'HMS *Glory*', as that worn by his daughter.

Burgess was charged that morning with murder and was brought before W S Gibson at an occasional court held at Hendon Town Hall. News had got around concerning the killing, and a crowd assembled outside the court to see the prisoner, who arrived in a closed brougham (carriage). Inside the courtroom the distraught Mr Fletcher had to be restrained after attempting to close with the prisoner. 'Leave me alone with that dog for a few minutes' he shouted as he was bustled away by police officers. The charges were that Burgess had been found loitering in Melrose Avenue for the supposed purpose of committing a felony; and that on or about 15 June, he 'did feloniously kill and slay Annie Fletcher, aged five, by stabbing her with a knife in a field near Edgware Brook'.

Burgess had made a detailed statement at Willeseden Green Police Station in which he admitted to choking the girl with a piece of muffler. This had been found at the scene of crime, and a matching piece was among the possessions Burgess had on him at time of arrest, along with the pocket-knife used to kill the child. Burgess probably confessed to sexually violating the girl also, though newspaper reports from the time tend merely to imply this, rather than state it clearly. Detective Inspector Wallace produced the bloodstained pocket-knife and the torn muffler as evidence in court.

Burgess had been labouring on the new Hampstead Garden Suburb and on the day prior to the killing had walked off-site after a row with his foreman. On the day of the murder he had left his digs in Childs Hill, ostensibly to go to work, and had never returned. He was described by the crime reporter for the *Hendon and Finchley Times* as 'a well set-up young fellow, clean shaven, with dark hair and eyes. He was collarless, with his shirt unfastened and his jacket collar upturned'.

Among the statements made to the police and read out at court there was a very important sighting of a man and girl by a tram driver, John Howard Frampton. He recalled dropping them both at Burnt Oak after the man rang the bell to alight. Following the hearing, and before being taken to Brixton Prison, Burgess was placed in an identity parade of eleven men. Here, the driver picked out Burgess as the man whom he had seen on the tram.

Burgess made three further appearances at court over the next fortnight. On each occasion large crowds formed with the intention of expressing their outrage at the crime, and this resulted in a strong police presence throughout. These appearances culminated in Burgess' committal on 9 July to the Central Criminal Court.

On 29 June the inquest was held at Hendon Town Hall. Dr Francis Danford Thomas conducted it. Mr A Munday was foreman of the jury. Once again, Mr Fletcher had to positively identify the victim as his daughter. I will spare the reader the facts of the post-mortem examination: suffice it to say that the report states there were numerous stab wounds on the body, and that the contents of the stomach revealed Annie Fletcher had eaten a hearty meal shortly before her death. Presumably, Burgess had picked her up some time that day and had made overtures of friendship towards her before taking her on a tram ride.

The case was heard on 21 July before the Lord Chief Justice, Lord Alverstone. The defence argued that Burgess was unfit to plea due to weakness of intellect, and the prosecution offered no objection to this claim.

Dr Dyer, Medical Officer at Brixton, was called to give evidence. He had known Burgess from some years previously, from Dartmoor Prison. According to his report Burgess came from a broken family, for his father had died in a railway accident, and as a result his mother gave way to drink and eventually died in prison. But there was no history of mental illness in the family. The report continued:

> *He is very dull, inclined to be morose, slow to appreciate and answer questions. Mentally unstable at times, with defective will power and memory and blunted moral sense. Burgess is impressionable and easily led by bad companions.*

Burgess is described as having led an aimless, nomadic and restless life. He had spent time in prison for wandering abroad, loitering with intent and setting fire to a mess room piano for some trivial reason during a brief period spent in the army. In the two or three years leading up to the killing the prisoner had experienced what he described as 'funny feelings' in his head, when he did not know what he was doing.

He further states that he did not know what he was doing all that day, that he had no intention whatever of committing this motiveless crime, and that afterwards he roamed about for two days and nights in the immediate vicinity, and on the third day 'thinking it was all a bad dream' re-visited the pond where the child's body was 'to see if it was a reality'.

According to Dr Dyer, Burgess '...did not know nor appreciate the nature and quality of his act. He was seized by a violent and paroxysmal fit of uncontrollable passion'.

John Patterson, a manager of the firm of Donald Robertson Paterson Ltd, testified that Burgess would have become familiar with the murder site through working as part of a team laying pipes in the area; some weeks before the murder he had been in attendance during the laying of a sewer running from the Silkstream to Bunn's Lane, Mill Hill.

The jury returned a verdict of insanity and the prisoner was ordered to be kept in custody at a criminal lunatic asylum 'until his Majesty's pleasure be known'.

CHAPTER 8

A Tale of Two Sweethearts

1911

'Yes, it is Baron.'

'Finchley is to-day a populous and popular suburb, a veritable network of streets, terraces and detached villa residences with their gardens, the latter often ample in size.' Thus Finchley is described in *Where to Live Round London,* in 1906. With its numerous transport links to London, its gravely subsoil assuring good drainage, and its low death rate, Finchley attracted many well-to-do house buyers.

Like in much of the country, April 1911 found Finchley in a state of considerable anticipation regarding the pending coronation of George V, due to take place that June. Various civic organizations, including the Finchley Urban District Council and the North Finchley Tradesmen's Association, held meetings in order to arrange celebrations in honour of the event. Despite the build-up of military power coupled with almost universal conscription taking place elsewhere in Europe, there was, as yet, no hint of the horrors that were to come in three years' time. All-in-all, Finchley must indeed have been a nice place to live in 1911.

One of the most pleasant streets in the district was Woodside Avenue, running to the west of, and parallel to, the Great North Road. Here there were plenty of the 'detached villa residences with gardens' described above. Woodside Avenue is still, today, a fine road, though some of the larger old houses have since been eaten up by small private estates. Near the north end of the road we find the North London Hospice and, situated on the front edge of its grounds, shading the

Woodside Avenue, North Finchley, c.1900. LBB

pavement in summer with dense foliage, there is an old horse chestnut. This very tree features significantly in the following account of yet another murder born of that lethal combination: alcohol and frustrated 'love'.

For over five and a half years twenty-two-year-old Alice Isabel Linford had worked as a chambermaid for John Dale Carr, a successful businessman, at Ryhope, his house in Woodside Avenue. Described as being of a happy disposition, Alice Linford had only two problems in her life: she was severely anaemic, a fact which became of issue in the court case following her eventual murder; and she was also trying to avoid her ex-sweetheart George Baron Pateman.

Thirty-three-year-old Pateman was something of a drunkard and ne'er-do-well. After a spell in the Royal Navy a few years previously, during which he had served on HMS *Warspite*, Pateman had tried to follow in his father's footsteps and establish himself as a gardener. He seems, however, to have made a poor show of it and was fired from a string of jobs for failing to turn up for work. He had been 'stepping out' (courting) with Alice for about three years, but the relationship had recently become distant, as the girl had been put off by Pateman's drinking. A trial separation to let things settle had been eased, supposedly, by Pateman's obtaining a job as gardener and groom at Wormington Rectory in Worcestershire. Yet, if Alice Linford's hope was that the physical distance between Pateman and herself would prove efficacious to the separation, she was to be proved cruelly wrong.

Pateman's father, Maurice, lodged with Alice Linford's family in Naylor Road, about half-a-mile to the north of Ryhope. He was gardener for John Carr and had planted numerous exotic species of tree and shrub behind the large brick house. The intertwining of the former sweethearts' respective families probably complicated any attempt at 'letting go' and making a clean break on the part of the young man.

By late April, Alice was getting on with her life and spending time going for walks with her elder sister, Rose. However, unknown to her, Pateman had walked out of the job at Wormington on 18 April and returned to London, staying with his sister Lily and brother-in-law at Cassio Villas in Puller Road, Barnet.

On the evening of Sunday, 23 April, he visited Ryhope to see Alice. The cook, Sarah Cole, told him Alice was not in, and Pateman asked her to keep his visit secret as he wanted to surprise her. He then left the house and crossed Woodside Avenue to wait in the shadows of a large fence that ran along the side of the road. Shortly afterwards Alice and Rose came walking along the opposite side of the road, on their way to Ryhope. Alice started when she noticed Pateman in the shadows and, thinking she had failed to recognize him – he was wearing a muffler and cap – Pateman crossed over to her and said, 'Yes, it is Baron.'

One imagines that Alice was unpleasantly shocked to see Pateman, but if so she tried to hide it. The three of them walked the short distance to Ryhope and, on departing, Pateman said 'Goodbye for the last time. I am going to end it all tonight.' Rose said, 'Oh no, Baron,' and advised him to go to his sister's house and get some sleep, to which he replied 'Curse that place. I don't want to go there again.' He then kissed Alice's hand, remarking 'You will hear the worst of me in the morning.'

After leaving Alice at Ryhope, Rose and Pateman walked together to Regent's Parade in North Finchley, where Rose had a small room. Pateman spent the night at his sister's despite his claim that he would never return to that place.

Over the next two days Pateman wrote several letters to Alice, in one of which he asked her to meet him at 7.30 on the coming Thursday evening at Barnet Church. Alice replied that she preferred not to, signing the letter affectionately. She later told her sister that she had grown afraid of Pateman after seeing him on the Sunday.

As previously mentioned, both Linford's family and Mr Pateman père lived in Naylor Road. Mr Linford was a much respected driver for the Metropolitan Electric Tramway Company. Alice often popped in to visit during her time off, and the family would sit around singing to the accompaniment of the piano in the drawing room. On the Thursday night, Alice Linford stayed there until about 10.30 before returning for night duty at Ryhope. Because she was anxious about meeting Pateman, his father offered to

The horse chestnut tree, Woodside Avenue, 2008. Peter Simon

accompany her on the half-mile walk back to the house. When they reached Woodside Lane, about 200 yards from Ryhope, Mr Pateman stood and waited while Alice walked towards the house. As she reached the gate Mr Pateman saw someone emerge from the shadows of a large horse chestnut growing close by and approach her. Thinking it was somebody from the house, Mr Pateman turned and set off back to Naylor Road. It was now about 11.15.

Inside Ryhope, the cook and housemaid were sitting in the ground floor kitchen making small talk when they saw Alice Linford rush past the window outside. The door flew open and she ran in holding her throat, from which blood was pouring. She fell on the hearthrug before the two women, whose screams brought Mr Carr running downstairs. A futile effort was made to staunch the bleeding from Alice's wounds and she quickly expired before the horrified witnesses. Mr Carr had telephoned for the police and for medical assistance, both of which arrived in due course. But Alice Linford was beyond help, and Detective Inspector Henry Brooks of Whetstone Police Station opened a murder inquiry.

A bloodstained razor was found on the pavement by the gate to Ryhope which, when tested for fingerprints, showed a hand print later identified as Pateman's. A search of Alice's room soon yielded the letters sent by Pateman, and Detective Inspector Brooks, accompanied by two other officers, travelled the three miles to Puller Road by motor car to visit Pateman. Arriving in the small hours, Brooks found Pateman asleep on a mattress with a rug thrown over him. Kicking the suspect awake, he told him to get dressed. Pateman was told the reason for the visit and cautioned, to which he replied 'I don't know anything about it.' He was then driven to Whetstone Police Station and questioned. The sleeves of Pateman's overcoat were noticed to have blood on them, and the article of clothing was immediately sent for analysis.

Over the next two days a detailed plan of the murder site – now stored at the Public Records Office in Kew – was drawn by PC Cook 405S. This includes the horse chestnut tree, mentioned above. It should be mentioned here that PC Cook was a first-rate draughtsman and had mapped the scene of

Puller Road, Barnet, 2008. Peter Simon

crime in the Annie Fletcher case (Ch. 7). He would go on to produce maps in the cases of George Sanger (Ch. 9) and Evelyn Goslett (Ch. 20).

The day after his arrest Pateman appeared at Highgate Court before Mr T Fraser Black. After verifying his address Pateman retreated into himself and appeared indifferent to the events taking place around him. Detective Inspector Brooks described the circumstances of the murder and explained how he had managed to track Pateman down. Pateman was then remanded into custody until the following Wednesday.

The post-mortem was carried out by a thirty-four-year-old pathologist, Dr Bernard J Spilsbury. Spilsbury had established a reputation for himself through his ground breaking forensic work in the Crippen case the previous year. Amongst other improvements he was to bring to 'the beastly science' (as forensics was known to its practitioners) was the presentation of concrete scientific evidence in court; before this written reports read out to the jury by counsel had been the norm. We will be hearing a lot more of Spilsbury in coming chapters.

Spilsbury concluded that the wound to Alice Linford's throat had been inflicted with great force by somebody standing behind her: the wound extended from the front of the throat almost to the right ear, the wind-pipe being completely severed. He agreed that the wound could have been produced by the razor found outside Ryhope.

The inquest opened at the Friern Barnet Council offices the following Tuesday before Dr George Cohen. The jury foreman was Mr W S Gibson, former chairman of Hendon District Council. Pateman refused the option of attending and was represented by Mr Thomas Charles, a solicitor based in Finchley. The first witness was Mr Linford, who had the sombre and unenviable duty of positively identifying the murder victim as his daughter. Mr Linford admitted that he had found Pateman an unsuitable sweetheart for Alice, and that he had, more than once insisted that Pateman leave her alone. In particular, he found Pateman's drinking and neglect of work abhorrent.

Rose Linford described in detail the events leading up to the murder, and Detective Inspector Brooks once again described the circumstances of the killing and subsequent arrest.

Perhaps most painfully, Maurice Pateman had to explain to the jury how his son had been besotted with Alice Linford and describe how he'd failed to accompany the girl to her front door when he walked her home that night.

Dr Cohen asked why Pateman and Linford had never got married during their time together and Mr Pateman explained that at one point arrangements had been made with the sexton at Totteridge. Anticipating his life with Alice, his son had bought furniture and paid a quarter's rent on a house. Unfortunately Alice had gone away to Wales at about that time with John Carr's daughter and, somehow, things had not been the same between them afterwards. Pateman had then sold the furniture and lived alone in the empty house for a while. One day he told his father that the house was dark and gloomy without Alice and that there was no brightness to 'look him in the face.' He had also said that if he did not have Alice he would not trouble about any other woman. With that Dr Cohen adjourned the inquest to await such information as would come to light as a result of the police investigation.

Alice Isabel Linford's funeral took place on the Thursday following her death. A service was held at St John's Church, Whetstone. Among the mourners were the father and mother, and the brothers and sisters of the deceased girl. Maurice Pateman was also in attendance. The coffin, carried into the church by employees of the Metropolitan Electric Tramways Company, was of polished elm, with brass fittings. After a sermon by the Reverend C J Goody the cortege set off for St Pancras cemetery in East Finchley. At nearly every house along the route the blinds were drawn as a sign of respect, and a large crowd assembled at Tally Ho Corner to watch the procession pass.

Pateman appeared once a week at Highgate over the next three weeks, on each occasion being remanded for seven days. On 19 May new evidence was presented to the court concerning the bloodstains which had been found on Pateman's overcoat. These had been sent to St Mary's Hospital where they had been subjected to a startling new form of analysis – the 'serum test' – by Dr William Henry Wilcox, senior scientific expert to the Home Office. A method was applied which enabled the analyst to distinguish between human blood and that of other mammals. Prior to this it had merely been possible to identify mammal blood as opposed to that of a bird or fish. This was the first time the new method had been used to provide evidence in a criminal case. Further, Dr Wilcox had been able to determine that the blood found on Pateman's coat had come from an anaemic person.

The coroner's inquest was resumed at the Friern Barnet Council Offices on 24 May. Pateman once again elected to not be present and was represented by Mr Charles. After hearing the evidence, which was largely corroborative of that already given at the magistrates' court, the jury concluded that Alice Isabel Linford had been wilfully murdered by George Baron Pateman.

The following week Pateman was committed to stand trial at the Central Criminal Court and was remanded in custody to await his fate.

The trial took place before Mr Justice Darling on 10 July. Pateman pleaded guilty to the charge. Pateman's father was called as a witness for the prosecution, but stated emphatically that he had not been able to recognize the person who had approached Alice on the night of the murder. The facts of the case otherwise not being in dispute, the jury had to decide whether the accused was sane or not at the time he committed the murder. Much was made of episodes of insanity in Pateman's family – his mother became violently deranged and had been confined to an asylum shortly before she died. It was also revealed that Pateman had suffered from syphilis during his time in the navy. Dr Dyer from Brixton Prison reported that he had been unable to find any indication of insanity in Pateman. Neither had he found the prisoner to be suffering from paranoia or delusions. Dr H Cole was called by the defence; he had been hired to give an independent medical assessment and had visited Pateman at Brixton the previous Saturday. Dr Cole stated that he had found the prisoner to be sullen and morose and disinclined to answer his questions. He said that Pateman had told him he had tried to commit suicide and he did not care what happened to him.

His Lordship, in summing up, drew attention to the progress of medical science as revealed by the case. He predicted a new era in which science would become the handmaiden of detection, rendering police work far easier and reducing crime statistics radically.

The jury found Pateman guilty of murder and, after hearing the death sentence, he walked unaided from the dock. Two weeks later Mr Charles presented an appeal to the Home Secretary, praying for a reprieve on the grounds of insanity. The Home Secretary concurred and advised the King to show clemency. This was granted, and Pateman began a sentence of penal servitude for life.

CHAPTER 9

A Circus Entrepreneur Takes His Final Bow

1911

*All police stations were warned, and many police
detachments were sent to aid in the search.*

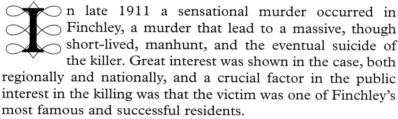n late 1911 a sensational murder occurred in Finchley, a murder that lead to a massive, though short-lived, manhunt, and the eventual suicide of the killer. Great interest was shown in the case, both regionally and nationally, and a crucial factor in the public interest in the killing was that the victim was one of Finchley's most famous and successful residents.

'Lord' George Sanger – the title was bogus – had made his fortune through establishing one of Britain's first touring circuses. Born in Newbury, Berkshire in 1824, Sanger came from a long line of showmen. Early on he showed an uncanny ability to train wild animals, beginning with two hares he taught to bang tambourines and fire miniature cannons, and over the years had made millions of pounds presenting spectacular shows up and down the country. Sanger's circus performed regularly before royalty: in 1898 he took his circus to Balmoral at the express wish of Queen Victoria, and was granted a personal audience with the ageing ruler. His displays were extravagant – on one memorable occasion he had over 700 people on stage together with numerous animals, including a whitewashed elephant. In 1901 he gave a show at Hendon in honour of the soldiers fighting the Boers in South Africa. Over one hundred specially trained horses enacted 'the dying and slain beasts upon the field of battle.' He was often called on to assist in the effects at state processions, and stage-

'Lord' George Sanger. LBB

managed many Lord Mayors' Shows.

The early days of the new century found Sanger beginning to struggle financially. A series of disastrous business moves, coupled with growing infirmity, lead him to retire in 1903 to Park Farm, a rambling affair situated on East End Road midway between Finchley Church End and East Finchley. The farm was a large one, its fields sloping to the south, off the Finchley boulder-clay. Here Sanger lived with his favourite animals, and for several years the locals were greeted with the site of several elephants and a somewhat ragged lion rambling through the meadows on the north bank of the Mutton Brook.

Sanger kept about him a small coterie of aides from his touring days, and employed a domestic staff drawn from the vicinity to service his needs. One of these, named George Cooper, was hired as Sanger's bailiff. Cooper moved into a small cottage across the road from Park Farm and Sanger developed a fondness for the man's young son, Herbert. The boy began working for the old man, and eventually gained access to his inner circle, attending Sanger nightly in the master bedroom and reading to him from the newspapers. He was often required to spend the whole night with Sanger, and was undoubtedly proud to possess such intimate access to the famous entrepreneur.

But as he entered into young manhood Herbert Cooper proved to be increasingly volatile. Two years prior to the events described below he had allowed a dog under his control to bite Ronald Robertson, a local veterinary surgeon who had accidentally strayed onto Sanger's property. Cooper had then struck Robertson's colleague, Dr William Cowper, unconscious with a large stick. Prosecuted at Hendon Court, he had his fine and costs covered by his employer. More recently Cooper had suffered a serious decline in status after an accusation of theft had been levelled at him by Sanger. He managed to keep his job, but was banned from attending so intimately upon his employer, his place being taken by another worker named Arthur Jackson. Cooper had also fallen into conflict with Jennie Beasley, a new employee at the farm, and developed a persecution complex as a result. Cooper felt that Jackson and Beasley had collaborated to turn George Sanger against him. Friends and family were later to testify that Cooper brooded on his fall from grace, and had seemed unhealthily preoccupied in the days following.

It now seems certain that Cooper was nursing murderous thoughts in his final days. Things came to a head on Tuesday, 28 November. At about six o'clock that evening Sanger was sitting in his drawing room, being read to by Harry Austin, a well-known circus bare-back rider while Arthur Jackson was in the kitchen reading quietly. Suddenly, Cooper burst into the house carrying an axe and razor and without warning attacked Jackson with the latter, slashing at his throat and inflicting a serious wound. Dropping the razor Cooper then entered the drawing room and set upon Sanger, hitting the man about the head with the axe. Austin, already alerted by Jackson's screams, threw himself at Cooper in an attempt to save the old showman, but not before several blows had been dealt to the victim's head. Sanger was wearing a felt cap and this was split in two, the axe embedding itself in Sanger's skull. Cooper then broke free of Austin's grasp and ran out of the farmhouse, leaving Sanger unconscious on the floor.

In the meanwhile Jackson had run out into the road and despite heavy bleeding from

Herbert Cooper. Author's collection

the wound to his throat he began shouting for help. Some shocked passers-by ran for help and the police and a doctor were summoned. On arrival they found the house in disarray and the attacker vanished. The still unconscious Sanger was removed to his bed: attempts were made to rouse him, but without success.

The police immediately instituted a search for the assailant: a pond in front of the farm was dragged, and groups of officers and farm-workers armed with sticks ranged far and wide for their quarry. Jackson and Austin informed the police as to the identity of the fugitive: 'All police stations were warned and many police detachments were sent to aid in the search' as the *Hendon and Finchley Times* put it.

The search increased in urgency later that evening after it was announced that Sanger had died as a result of the attack. Every attempt had been made to save his life but he passed away shortly before eleven o'clock without regaining consciousness. Cooper was now wanted for murder.

The St Marylebone cemetery, on East End Road, was checked closely while dog teams scoured the woods towards Hampstead. Witnesses came forward claiming to have seen Cooper crossing the railway bridge in Church Lane, East Finchley, and cycling towards London on the Great North Road. These leads were followed up but it was all to no avail; when morning came there was still no trace of the wanted man. Warnings were then telegraphed to all ports alerting them to the possibility of the fugitive's leaving the country.

There was a great surge of grief in Finchley at the news of Sanger's death. He had been a charismatic presence in the neighbourhood, his nightly watering of the elephants at the pond by East End Road adjacent to the farm always guaranteeing to attract a crowd. Both the *Hendon and Finchley Times* and the *Finchley Press* reported at length on the murder, and included potted histories of the circus man in their respective articles. The following days saw crowds form outside Park Farm and multitudes of photographers assembled, photographing everything in sight, including the skull of a large elephant which Sanger had been forced to shoot two years earlier and had placed above the entrance to the farmhouse. In the meantime reports – all false – flooded in to Scotland Yard of sightings of Cooper. People who had known the man also contacted the police with suggestions as to where he may have been hiding, but they were wrong: Cooper was much closer to the scene of crime than anybody realised, and he could no-longer be counted among the living.

In those days a railway line ran between Highgate and Alexandra Palace: its course is still visible today in parts of Highgate Wood, and in a footpath built over the route, close to 'Ally-Pally'. On the evening of the day following the killing a winter mist descended over the area and neither the train drivers, nor the workmen maintaining the permanent way early the next morning, could see further than a few yards. At about 7.20 am a train stopped momentarily to allow a signal to change. A passenger glancing out the window noticed a pair of legs protruding from below the train. The alert was given and police officers and railway officials made their way along the track. A body, neatly decapitated, was found and quickly identified as Cooper's. A considerable amount of money was found in the dead man's pocket together with a watch, a diary and a letter addressed to his father in which he admitted to murdering Sanger, claiming that the perceived conspiracy against him had 'turned my brain'. He ended the letter 'Your broken-hearted son'. In his diary was found the following note addressed to his brother Harry:

> *I am sorry things should have come to this. No one knows what it is I have gone through. What I have told you was the truth, and Mr George turned like he did after all this time I have been with him. I could not stand it. I have blamed Jennie Beasley for all. Let her think it over. Goodbye.*

The inquests upon the deaths of Sanger and Cooper were held at Friern Barnet Urban Council on 2 December before Dr George Cohen. After hearing the evidence the jury returned a verdict of wilful murder against Cooper. He was found also to have committed suicide while temporarily insane.

Sanger was buried with ostentatious display at Margate, thousands of people lining the streets between Margate West station and the cemetery to pay their last respects to the great showman. Today, Park Farm is long gone, eaten up by the need for housing. Park Avenue, a residential street, is all that remains to remind us of the events that occurred in November 1911.

CHAPTER 10

The West Hendon Shootings

1911 & 1913

I ask, was it any wonder that such anxiety was too much for the brain, and that the mental power was cast from its throne?

The College Farm shooting serves to remind us that 'gun crime' is not a solely recent phenomenon. And lest we think that case was a mere anomaly, an early trial run for the almost casual gun law of our own age, we need look no further than Hendon in the years 1911 and 1913 in order to be disabused of such a view. For, in the space of these two years, there were three fatal shootings in that unhappy place, two of them occurring within a fortnight of each other.

But before we proceed, a new arrival in Hendon needs also to be considered at this point. In April 1910 two airmen, Claude Grahame-White and Louis Paulhan, held a race to be the first to fly from London to Manchester. A lot was at stake, as the *Daily Mail* had offered £10,000 to the victor. Paulhan, who in fact went on to win the race, assembled his aircraft in a field situated between the Midland Railway and Edgware Road, near Colindale. Later, other airmen used the same plot, a small shed being erected for storing the aircraft, and Hendon Aerodrome was born. The aerodrome expanded over the next few years: engineering plants catering for the needs of the aircraft were opened in the area, and a large workforce was housed close by. Eventually, Hendon became the home of British aeronautics and will be a background presence in several chapters to come. Further, the first killing covered in *this* chapter actually took place at the aerodrome.

In August 1911 a young Frenchman, Francois Hanot, aged thirty, arrived at Hendon. Hanot was clearly enthralled with the idea of being a pilot, and he enrolled at the Blériot School

A young French airman at Hendon, c.1912. LBB

of Aviation – owned by Grahame-White – paying £50 for tuition and a £49 deposit. Perhaps Hanot envisaged taking to the air in a couple of days – the events described here certainly paint a picture of a man who was additionally prone to flights of fancy. However, Hanot seems to have lacked any especial aptitude for flying; instead, he had to attend classes on theory and mechanics along with the other students, and progress was far slower than he had imagined it would be.

He resented the attention the aircraft mechanics gave him, with regard to his safety, brushing their concerns aside, and claiming he didn't need their assistance as he knew what flying was all about. In particular, he developed a loathing for his flying instructor, Paul Maurice Petit Pierre, a thirty-one-year-old fellow Frenchman. By the end of his first week Hanot, despite managing to finally fly his aircraft on a circuit around the aerodrome, was seething with resentment.

It was 5.15 pm on Saturday, 19 August. A well-known flyer, M Gustav Hamel, had just taken off from Hendon on a flight to Southend – gripping stuff in 1911 – and a sizeable number of people were gathered near the aircraft hangers to watch. The general atmosphere must have been one of excitement and adventure, but Hanot was in no mood to join in. Instead, he approached Norbert Chereau, the manager of the Blériot School, and demanded the return of both his fee and his deposit. According to Hanot, he had not received the training he had expected and a full refund was in order. The manager explained that this was impossible and several other members of staff became drawn into the dispute, castigating Hanot for his impatience. In particular, the hated Petit Pierre joined the two men and supported the manager in his decision.

'You won't return me my money then?' Hanot had asked.

'No. That would be unreasonable,' Chereau replied, 'as you have no serious complaint to make.'

At this, Hanot seemed to calm down and even shook hands with Petit Pierre. They then stood with the crowd for about fifteen minutes, watching the last planes of the day taking off and landing and then, as rain started to fall, the small crowd began to disperse, seeking shelter in some sheds.

It was at this point that Hanot suddenly whipped out a handgun, later identified as a Mauser automatic pistol, and opened fire at the group standing around him. Great consternation was caused by the fusillade and the crowd scattered for cover. A young Englishman named Inglis ran towards Hanot in an attempt to disarm the distraught Frenchman, but he proved to be too late.

One of Hanot's bullets struck Petit Pierre in the thigh, and he collapsed with blood spurting from the wound. Inglis threw himself onto Hanot, and a number of other people rushed forward to help restrain the crazed man. Hanot managed to struggle free and then turned the gun on himself, firing three shots into his body and falling to the ground before the horrified bystanders.

By chance, Dr AC White was in attendance at the aerodrome, and he was summoned immediately, blankets being placed on the two badly injured men. Dr White saw to the needs of Petit Pierre and then approached Hanot, together with Chereau.

Hanot was still conscious and, when asked why he'd done it, replied 'I shot the man because he would not give me my money back.' Chereau then asked him where his friends were and he replied, 'I have no friends. I have only you.' Hanot requested that his pocket book, which contained twenty pounds in gold and notes, and his gold watch, should be forwarded to the policeman, PC Cooper, with whom he had lodged in Colindale.

If Chereau and Dr White thought that events had now run their course, and that Hanot had effectively been disarmed, they were about to be disillusioned; Hanot suddenly pulled out a concealed razor and slashed his own throat, compounding his already dreadful injuries.

Petit Pierre was initially moved to the Central London Sick Asylum, in Colindale, but later both he and Hanot were transferred to St Mary's Hospital, Paddington. Hanot died from his injuries at about one o'clock the following afternoon, Petit Pierre expiring about an hour later.

The inquest was held at Paddington the following Tuesday under Dr Danford Thomas. George Jules Petit Pierre identified the body of his brother and stated that, as far as he knew, he'd had no enemies. Norbert Chereau described the events of Saturday evening: 'To me,' he said 'it seemed Hanot had an imaginary grievance. He wrote to me on Friday that he had been told that we would not teach him properly at the school, and that he did not believe that he could learn what was necessary.' Chereau described how Hanot had been taught the basic principles of flight by Petit Pierre but had then complained that his instructor was not a fully qualified pilot.

Detective Inspector Henry Brooks described how he had visited Hanot's lodgings and found two boxes of cartridges identical to those fired at Hendon Aerodrome. Pupils from the school expressed satisfaction with Petit Pierre's instruction – Hanot, according to one pupil, had appeared to be anxious to fly after two days' instruction.

The jury found that Hanot murdered Petit Pierre and then committed suicide. Petit Pierre was buried a few days later at the Hendon Park Cemetery. Among the floral tributes was one in the form of an aeroplane, small white flowers being used. This was from the staff, pilots and pupils of the Grahame-White Aviation Company.

Hendon played host to two more killings little more than eighteen months later. And, once again, guns were the instrument of murder.

It was early 1913 and Albert Sherring, thirty-four, and his wife, Beatrice, twenty-two, had been married for less than a year. Unfortunately Mr Sherring was a heavy drinker and things had not gone well between them: despite having had a child the previous June, they separated in August amidst much acrimony. Beatrice Sherring remained in the flat they'd once shared, which was located in her mother's house in Wilberforce Road, West Hendon, close to the Schweppes factory. Mr Sherring went to stay with *his* mother a short distance away, at Deerfield Cottages (since demolished to make way for the M1 Motorway).

Beatrice Sherring was clearly not a woman to place her life on hold just because of a separation: she obtained a job in a florist's shop in newly developing Golders Green, where her sister Violet Fletcher also worked, and took the motor omnibus daily to and from work. She had also begun 'walking out' with a new man, a butcher's assistant named Leonard Aggis, also from Golders Green.

Albert Sherring never saw his wife, even by appointment, though he persistently harassed her, entering trams on which she travelled, or visiting her at the flower shop. Presumably, he was infuriated by her racy lifestyle. Several weeks previously he had 'run into her' and her sister in Cricklewood and followed them home. He confronted Beatrice Sherring and Aggis in Childs Hill at the end of February, claiming to his brother, William, that he had chased his rival down Cricklewood Lane. By chance, he met Aggis two days later in the *Prince Albert*

Wilberforce Road, c.1900. LBB

public house in Golders Green Road, near what is now the North Circular Road. Aggis assured Sherring that he had not realised Beatrice Sherring was married, but this did not satisfy him. Sherring brooded on how his wife seemed to be getting on fine without him and, eventually, began to plot revenge. The following weekend he took out a gun licence. He also secretly obtained a gun from an unknown source, a revolver of American make, with five chambers.

At lunchtime on Monday, 3 March Sherring stood by the pond at the Burroughs, Hendon, and waited until he saw the motor omnibus pass with Beatrice and Violet aboard. Mounting his bicycle, he followed the bus as it descended Station Road towards West Hendon, overtaking the sisters as they alighted at Wilberforce Road.

Leaning his bicycle against a wall he confronted the two women outside their home. 'How do you like this?' he said, as he drew the revolver from beneath his jacket. He fired at his wife, two bullets striking her in the chest with devastating effect. In a futile attempt to protect her sister, Violet Fletcher threw her Dorothy bag at Sherring whereupon he fired at her, fortunately missing; the bullet passed so close to her that it left a thin line of powder on her face. Not satisfied with this vile deed, Sherring then stepped up to his wife as she lay on the ground. He placed the barrel of the revolver to her left ear and fired again. He then put the gun to his own head, fired and dropped dead on the pavement.

By now, alerted by Violet Fletcher's screams and the sound of pistol shots, people were hurrying to offer assistance. One of these, Robert Frown, a carman, had been riding nearby on the high dickey of a carriage. He had to rein in his horse, which had been much alarmed by the report from the gun. He ran to where the dead pair lay and, mounting Sherring's bicycle, sped off to fetch the police.

Meanwhile, a neighbour had run into the Fletchers' house shouting, 'Something has happened to "Beat", but don't let Mrs Fletcher come.' But hearing this, Mrs Fletcher did go outside and found her daughter lying dead in a pool of blood. Beatrice's body was carried inside, while Sherring's was left on the pavement. A local doctor, Dr Bethune, arrived shortly afterwards. He declared Beatrice Sherring dead, privately noting that her death must have been instantaneous. He also examined Sherring's corpse, concluding that death was due to a gun shot wound to the head. Later, both bodies were removed to the mortuary at Hendon Town Hall. Finally, an hour after the shooting, the police arrived to find the bodies already gone. Their tardiness was to later provoke some well-earned criticism.

Painful revelations were made at the inquest, held before Dr George Cohen on 6 March. Beatrice Sherring's death was considered first, followed by an inquiry into that of her husband. A large crowd, among who were many neighbours and friends of the deceased, assembled for the hearing. A somewhat embarrassed Divisional Inspector Barrel accompanied by Station Sergeant Davies and Detective Sergeant Luxton, represented the police authorities.

Beatrice Sherring's mother bravely refused the offer of a seat and gave her evidence standing. As she stood, holding her orphaned grandchild in her arms, she told the inquest she had last seen her daughter on the day of the shooting, and had kissed her goodbye as Beatrice left for work. She then described the relationship between her daughter and Sherring, and the events of the previous Monday.

Violet Fletcher was able to provide the inquest with the details of Sherring's conduct in the weeks preceding the tragedy, and an account of the actual shooting in Wilberforce Road. Several other witnesses also gave accounts of the incident, all agreeing as to the exact sequence of events.

Sherring's brother, William, told of how he had been worried for Albert in recent weeks: Albert Sherring had been particularly upset by seeing his wife with another man. The previous July the two brothers had visited Wilberforce Road together to collect Albert's shaving kit. Albert Sherring had told Mrs Fletcher that if he and his wife couldn't live together he would take the baby. Mrs Fletcher had replied, 'The child is not yours and you shan't have it, and I can prove it.' A serious argument then broke out in the hallway of the house, and Albert Sherring and Beatrice's younger brother had come to blows.

Leonard Aggis gave his version of events, describing his meeting with Albert Sherring in the *Prince Albert*. Dr Bethune described the injuries to Beatrice Sherring; the two bullet wounds in the chest, and the other to the head.

In summing up, Dr Cohen said that it was a particularly sad case. He advised the jury to reach a verdict of wilful murder against Albert Sherring, which they did, without hesitation.

The inquest into Albert Sherring's death next took place. The only additional witness was William McKie, who had been Sherring's foreman on a building site in Golders Green. He stated how Sherring had told him only a few days previously about running into his wife with another man; Sherring had seemed very upset, and had not turned up for work the next day, and had even failed to collect his wages on the Saturday.

The coroner instructed the jury that there was no doubt as to the cause of death in this case. However, they had to state what, in their opinion, had been the state of mind of the deceased. If there was insufficient evidence to indicate Sherring's state of mind then they should reach a verdict of *felo de se*. If they wished to say – as he thought they had every reason for saying – that his mind was not quite sound, then they could return a verdict that he had killed himself whilst of unsound mind. The jury consulted together for a few minutes and gave their verdict: that Albert Sherring had killed himself with a self-inflicted wound to the head, and that at the time he killed himself, deceased was of unsound mind.

Impressive scenes attended the funerals of Mr and Mrs Sherring the following weekend. Perhaps reflecting the values of the age, a greater degree of public sympathy was shown for Mr Sherring. Large crowds showed up for the service, which was held at West Hendon Baptist Hall, close to Wilberforce Road, on Saturday morning. The Reverend W J Fox conducted the service, and gave a long sermon on the difficulties faced by the deceased in his final days. After describing in somewhat couched terms the pain, induced by the presumed betrayal, under which Albert Sherring had laboured, he then posed the following question:

> *I ask, was it any wonder that such anxiety was too much for the brain, and that the mental power was cast from its throne, and instead of that power holding the reins of life and guiding that life in the right direction, the throne was vacant, and the steering gear of life was out of all control.*

The body was then transferred to St Mary's Church, Hendon, where it was interred in the churchyard.

Beatrice Sherring's funeral was, by comparison, a low-key affair. She was buried at the Hendon Park cemetery on Monday morning, the location having been kept a secret. Several police officers were stationed in Wilberforce Road as the funeral cortege departed, as there were fears that the relatives of the deceased woman would be subjected to public demonstration. Mercifully, only a few dozen people flocked to Wilberforce Road, and both the departure and the funeral passed off quietly.

If the Sherring affair caused the residents of West Hendon to pause and contemplate the nature of the society in which they lived, perhaps concluding that they had now had their share of such tragedies, they were about to be proved cruelly wrong. Before the month was out, West Hendon was once more the scene of a shooting – this time resulting in injury to the brother of the intended victim and the suicide of the malefactor. And again it involved a couple, separated and with a child, and yet again alcohol was cited as a cause of the separation.

On Tuesday, 1 April, Charles Edmund West, thirty-five, banged on the door of the house in St John's Parade, West Hendon Broadway, where his estranged wife, Florence, was staying with her mother. His mother-in-law, Mrs Isabella Travers opened the door and was greeted with the sight of West pointing a small revolver directly at her. Thinking quickly, Mrs Travers ducked and ran to the kitchen, barring the door by placing a poker beneath it. She yelled loudly for the police and her son, Adolphus, alerted by her shouts, ran down the stairs just in time to see West walking away along the Broadway.

Travers followed closely behind, calling on West to stop as he wanted a word with him. As yet he was unaware that West had a revolver on his person. He merely wanted to 'have it out' with his brother-in-law concerning what was the latest in a long line of unwanted visits to the family home.

Mrs West had already had a court order issued against her husband for threatening behaviour, but West had ignored the summons and failed to turn up to court. Now, as Travers

West Hendon Broadway, c.1910. LBB

closed on his family's persecutor, West turned round, pulled out his gun and fired, the bullet hitting Travers in the arm. Understandably shocked, and probably with images of the Sherring incident flashing through his mind, Travers ran into Mr Thomas' dairy shop, where he besought the assistant to telephone for the police. This she tried to do, but the telephone system was still in its infancy in 1913 and all the lines were in use. Travers then glanced round and saw West lurching away across the Broadway in the direction of the Welsh Harp. Regaining his composure, Travers left the dairy and followed West, once more shouting, 'Stop that man!' As he began to catch up with West, that man fired another shot at him and he backed off. Once more West walked on ahead until, at the junction of Stanley Road with the Broadway he stopped. Placing the gun in his own mouth he pulled the trigger. A loud click sounded – the gun had misfired. West then opened the revolver and coolly examined it for a moment before closing it and again placing the revolver in his mouth. He pulled the trigger twice in rapid succession and this time the gun fired, the second bullet passing through the roof of his mouth and blowing the top of his head wide apart.

A crowd quickly gathered about the injured man as he lay on the pavement, his head leaning against a lamppost. Despite the fact that his brains were oozing out of his head he was still alive, and a cab was hastily summoned to take him to St Mary's Hospital, Paddington. Here he died two days later. Finally, over thirty minutes after the shooting, the police arrived, finding little more than a pool of blood and some fragments of West's head to keep them occupied.

The jury at the coroner's inquest, held in Paddington before Mr C Luxmore-Drew, heard a story similar to that presented to Dr George Cohen at Hendon less than a month earlier. Once again the jury returned a verdict of suicide whilst of unsound mind.

One can well imagine the consternation in Hendon upon hearing news of this second incident. While clearly a copy-cat shooting, inspired by the Sherring case, West's suicide and his shooting of Travers might well have caused the local population to ponder on whether there wasn't some deep malaise at work in the community, perhaps a moral laxity, coupled with an all-to-easy ability to purchase firearms. Strangely, nobody seems to have considered the role alcoholism played in these two cases.

What *was* of concern was the slack response by the constabulary to both the Sherring and the Travers/West incidents. As we have seen, on each occasion the police arrived later than either the doctor, or the transport used to convey the injured to hospital, the dead to the mortuary. The anxiety this awareness caused among the residents of Hendon is best summed up by this excerpt from a letter published in the *Hendon and Finchley Times* on 4 April:

> *We have had within a fortnight two terrible tragedies enacted in our midst, and on each occasion it has been some considerable time before the police have arrived. We have police from two distinct divisions, namely Willesden and Hendon, and it is up to the rate-payers to agitate for some arrangement to be made between the two divisions to always have at least one policeman on duty in the Broadway.*

The writer then went on to complain how all the public telephones had been in use on the day of the second shooting and that the police telephone box located on the Broadway had no telephone!

CHAPTER 11

The Hendon Wine Shop Murder

1919

He wanted to do the dirty on me.

The modern day reader will be shocked by the following account, for not only is the violence described of an extreme nature, but the attitude of both the police and the trial judge towards the victim, a homosexual, is callous indeed.

During World War One, Hendon Aerodrome grew to become the centre of British aircraft production. Stimulated by the forces' demand for new models, numerous aircraft factories sprang up around the aerodrome, and also in Cricklewood and the Hyde. Housing complexes, such as Aeroville in Colindale, were erected for the new population of skilled workers. Large numbers of additional workers arrived at Colindale each morning by tram. There were inevitable cutbacks when the war ended but aviation had by now firmly established itself in the area. The RAF would take over the running of the aerodrome in 1922, eventually selling off the site for housing in 1970.

The period immediately following the War was a difficult one for young men: a surplus of male workers caused by demobilisation led to great competition for labour, and the factories serving the aerodrome attracted many a lad seeking work in the new industry. It was one of these, Arthur John Biggin, aged eighteen, who alighted from a tram on Edgware Road at Colindale one day in June 1919. Straightening his hat he quickly crossed the main road; he was in a hurry because he had an appointment for an interview at the Integral Propeller Company.

Biggin was the product of a privileged upbringing; his father was a well-known and successful businessman and engineer in Sheffield. Perhaps wearying of his role as the scion of a wealthy family with all its attendant expectations, and intent on making his own way in the world, Arthur Biggin had left his young wife in Sheffield and come down to London the previous year. He rented the ground floor of a house in Fordwych Road, Cricklewood and drifted from job to job, attempting to find his feet. He now wanted to establish himself in the exciting new world of powered flight, perhaps seeking to emulate his father's successful career in engineering.

The walk from the Edgware Road to the factory took Biggin down Colindale Avenue. Fearing that he had lost his way, Biggin approached a man to ask for directions. To his consternation the gentleman ignored his request and instead asked 'Would you care to be my guest for a few moments?' For reasons that are not clear Biggin accepted the man's invitation and accompanied him into the Hendon Wine Store close by. Following his new companion into a room behind the shop counter Biggin sat down and accepted the offer of a cigarette and a glass of port from the tall grey-haired man.

John Thomas Gregory was manager of the Hendon Wine Store. The fifty-nine-year-old lived in Ealing with his daughter but would often stay the night at the Wine Store, sparing himself the long journey to and from work. The owners of the Wine Store knew of the nights spent at the shop; this suited them for reasons of security. The arrangement suited John Gregory also – he was an active homosexual at a time when to be such was to break the law, and the premises provided the safety and privacy he needed for the pursuit of his interests.

Apparently, none of this was as yet known to Biggin, who finished his port, made his excuses and left. On the way out he promised to look Gregory up at some future time. He then rushed off, late for his interview.

Needless to say, Biggin failed to secure the job, but a week or so later he turned up at Colindale Avenue again. Unfortunately the shop was closed, and Gregory not in. Biggin asked for pen and paper at a local stationer's shop and wrote a note for Gregory which he posted through the front door:

Dear old Bean — I called this morning and found you were out. Was very disappointed. Will call later in the week.

Signed
'Cyril.'

Several days later Biggin ran into Gregory by chance on a tram in town. The conversation which followed was initially friendly. Gregory suggested that Biggin come to the wine shop the next day and collect some bottles of beer and wine to take home with him. He told Biggin to bring a suitcase with him, the better to carry the bottles in. Gregory then made what was described later, in court, as 'an improper suggestion' to the young man, who reacted by stating in no uncertain terms that he wasn't interested. The two men then laughed off Gregory's approach and Biggin agreed to call the following day to collect the drink.

Shortly before this, Biggin had moved from Fordwych Road, taking a room at the YMCA in Tottenham Court Road. That night he discussed Gregory's offer of beer and wine with his new cohabitants and they agreed that it would be a good idea for him to visit Gregory and collect the free drink. The next morning, it was Friday, 4 July, he borrowed a suitcase from a friend named Bowles and set off for Colindale.

A surprise awaited Biggin when he arrived at the Wine Store. Gregory ushered him into the back of the shop where a table had been laid for a meal. Plates were spread, each loaded with choice meats. Pickle jars and dishes of tomatoes intermingled with bottles of select wine and spirit: clearly Gregory intended to treat the young man.

Biggin was taken aback by the lavish display; maybe he'd hoped to load up the suitcase as quickly as possible and leave. He explained to Gregory that he couldn't stay long and asked him to collect some bottles from the store room to take with him. Gregory was persuasive however and, before long, Biggin had joined him at the table, the two chatting amiably as they ate and drank.

What happened next is based solely on Biggin's testimony. After finishing the meal the two of them went and sat in the parlour. Godfey excused himself for a moment and returned with a bottle containing a reddish yellow liquid. He offered some to Biggin who, though unused to drink, was as yet not overly intoxicated. 'I had no other option but to drink it,' Biggin later told the court. 'It was heavy and sickly with a bitter-sweet taste and after I'd drunk it my head seemed to go heavy and dizzy.' It was at this point that Gregory renewed his overtures: 'He began to tell me some filthy tales,' was how Biggin later put it. Perhaps he had been naïve to expect Gregory to do otherwise; perhaps he had decided to lead Gregory on, the better to wheedle some free drink out of him. Either way, Biggin now began to feel that he was out of his depth.

Biggin continued to refuse Gregory's increasingly overt demands. Suddenly Gregory got up, picked up a steel poker and approached Biggin saying: 'You young viper, you won't, will you? Then I will make you.' He then put his hand in Biggin's trousers pocket. This was too much for Biggin, who backed off, telling Gregory that he wanted to leave. According to Biggin, Gregory 'seemed to become raving mad'. He rushed at Biggin and aimed a terrific blow at his head with the poker. Terrified, Biggin ducked and threw himself on Gregory, the better to defend himself.

Gregory was a very powerful man and, as the two men struggled, he seemed to be gaining the upper hand. Panicking, Biggin grabbed a pair of fire tongs and hit Gregory hard on the head knocking him to the floor. He then picked up the steel poker and struck Gregory several times with such ferocity that the instrument was bent out of shape. He also picked up a lemonade bottle and struck Gregory with it. Gregory lay groaning on the carpet, blood pouring from his head. At that moment Biggin heard voices coming outside, from Colindale Avenue. He went to the window looking out onto the street and saw several people staring through at him. Drawing the curtains – he left a smear of blood on the glass – he looked round at Gregory, still laying on the floor, and decided he had to escape. Passing through the kitchen at the back of the store, Biggin crossed the garden and climbed over a fence into a street running off Colindale Avenue. Nobody was there and

Biggin quickly departed. Clearly shaken by his experience and splattered with blood, he approached a man leaning against a stile and asked for a cigarette. He then threaded through to West Hendon, leaving Edgware Road via Deerfield Cottages and caught a bus to Golders Green. From there he travelled to Tottenham Court Road. The next day he borrowed £2 from a friend and took the train back to Sheffield, intending to lie low until he had decided what to do.

The people Biggin had seen from the window of the Hendon Wine Store were a number of workers from the nearby Titanine-Emaillite Factory. They had been heading towards Edgware Road to take the tram home at the end of their shift. Alarmed by thudding noises and the sound of smashing glass coming from the store, a group of workers looked over at the window of the building just in time to see somebody draw the curtains, leaving a smear of blood on the glass. One of the workers ran off to Edgware Road and summoned PC Cooper, who was directing traffic. By the time Cooper got to the Wine Store a crowd had assembled and several men were peering through the letterbox. Finding the door locked Cooper prised open the window and looking in, saw a badly injured man lying on his back near the fireplace. There were blood splashes on the wall of the room and a large amount of debris scattered about the floor. Rushing to the injured man's aid, Cooper climbed through the window, but Gregory expired within seconds of the PC's reaching him.

Within half-an-hour Divisional Inspector Duggan, Detective Inspector McEvoy and Detective Sergeants Luxton, Askew and Burgess had arrived. They were joined shortly afterwards by Chief Detective Inspector Neil from Scotland Yard.

Gregory's violent death caused a considerable stir in Hendon, the *Hendon and Finchley Times* commenting on the killing thus:

> *As far as the district served by the Hendon and Finchley Times is concerned, Hendon has of late years been free from these dastardly outrages. In 1913 three crimes were committed in one year, but since that date nothing of a like character has taken place.*

The paper then went on to remind its readership of the events in West Hendon described in the previous chapter of this book. The third killing occurred in Marsh Lane in Stanmore, outside our area, and need not concern us here.

When the inquest opened on the deadman at Hendon Town Hall, Dr George Cohen insisted that some of the evidence be heard *in camera*, and the public and press where accordingly ushered outside. It is probable that this involved evidence pertaining to Gregory's sexuality. Sybil Gregory, the victim's daughter, told the inquest that the suitcase was not her father's. Several witnesses, including the man at the stile who gave Biggin a cigarette shortly after his escape, attempted to give a full description. None of them seemed able to do so, though several mentioned his seeming ill-at-ease and being spattered with blood. It was concluded that the perpetrator was about five-foot-eight in height, clean shaven, of medium build and wore a grey trilby and smart trousers, with permanent turn-ups.

Dr F W Andrew, who had carried out the post-mortem, described the victim's injuries: these had probably been caused by the broken bottle, poker and tongs found at the scene of crime. Gregory's skull had been fractured. There were five wounds, any one of which would have rendered him immediately unconscious. Four of these, he considered, had been inflicted while Gregory was on the ground.

The jury returned a verdict of murder against a person or persons unknown, and Dr Cohen expressed regret that the man responsible for Gregory's death wasn't before them.

The police had initially thought that Gregory had stumbled across a burglary. This theory was discounted almost immediately: the table set for two and the half-emptied glasses told another tale. Officers searching the premises quickly found the suitcase Biggin had brought with him. They were intrigued by the initials J W B inscribed on it, and made sure the papers reported on the find. This was read by the suitcase's owner who contacted the police. Other guests at the YMCA reported the state Biggin was in on the evening of the murder. The police were now on Biggin's trail.

Biggin read of Gregory's death in the national newspapers and, aware that it was only a matter of time before he was arrested on the capital charge, decided to end it all. On Friday, 11 July he was found unconscious in Whitley Wood in Sheffield. He was rushed to hospital where he was found to be suffering from the effects of Potassium Cyanide poisoning. Fortunately he had taken only a small amount. Nursed back to health, he was then interviewed by Detective Inspector Dyson of the Sheffield police. His identity being established, Biggin was handed over to Chief Detective Inspector Neil who had travelled up to Sheffield by the night train. He was then brought back by train to London and held at Hendon Police Station. Here he made a long statement in which he admitted to killing Gregory. Biggin was adamant that he had merely tried to defend himself in a terrifying situation and claimed that he had sought to evade justice because he had felt that no one would listen to him.

Biggin came up before the magistrates at Hendon Police Court on Monday, 14 July. Described in the *Hendon and Finchley Times* as looking very pale, he was granted permission by the magistrates, J M McGrath and G Gale Thomas to remain seated throughout. His statement was read to the court and Biggin reserved his defence. This being an occasional court, held specifically to remand him, he was placed in custody to appear before a full bench the following Friday.

The police continued their inquiries and interviewed several young men who came forward after reading of the case in the press. None of this was apparent when Biggin next appeared before the magistrates. A large crowd assembled outside the courthouse, and stretched some distance along the pavement to either side of the building, waiting to catch a glimpse of the accused. Mr A K Carlyon presided over a full bench and Biggin was called to answer to the charge of murder. After reading the prisoner's statement to the court, the representative for the prosecution, Eustace Fulton outlined the basis of the accusation:

If his statement be true on July 3rd he was aware of the sort of person he alleged Gregory to be, and for what purpose he was being invited to the wine shop. Therefore he knew quite well when he went there on July 4th the purpose for which he was asked to

*go, and either consented or was prepared to pretend for the
purpose of getting wine.*

The number of blows which were delivered was quite
unnecessary to protect the accused from assault, Fulton
pointed out. Any one would have been sufficient.

*Under our law a man is entitled to use only such force as is
necessary to protect himself. If he exceeded that force, and in
exceeding it killed a man he would be guilty of willful murder.*

With this Biggin was committed to stand trial at the Old
Bailey.

The case came up on 15 September before the seventy-year-
old Mr Justice Darling. Biggin pleaded not guilty. That Biggin
had dealt the fatal blow to Gregory was not in doubt. The
issue was the circumstances under which the defendant had so
acted. During the trial Sir Richard Muir, for the Crown,
subjected Biggin to a severe cross-examination, accusing him
of attempting to use Gregory's interest in him to his own
advantage. If Biggin had gone to the Hendon Wine Store

Hendon Court House c.1920. LBB

knowing of Gregory's intentions but himself intending to use this to trick the older man to his own advantage, didn't it follow that he would be prepared to resort to violence should circumstances dictate? At one point Justice Darling expressed interest in the note headed 'My old Bean' and asked the defendant the meaning of the term, Biggin replying that it was army slang.

If things looked bad for Biggin then help was to come from an unexpected quarter: the defence called Police Sergeant Bubear, of the Devon Constabulary who testified that in 1912 he had been ordered to keep Gregory – who had owned a wine shop in the area – under close observation on account of his reputation. He did so, but although he received information on Gregory's behaviour almost daily, he could get no proof. No less than six male witnesses were then called, all of whom testified that John Thomas Gregory had made near-violent attempts to seduce them. One of them, a flight sergeant in the RAF, admitted to throwing a bottle at Gregory in order to warn him off. 'He wanted to do the dirty on me,' another exclaimed. The jury was clearly shocked by this evidence.

In summing up, Justice Darling reminded the jury that there were legal reasons which justified the taking of human life. There were not many cases in which they applied, but one of these was the need for a man to defend himself against a felony being committed against his own person. The jury might feel in this case that the prisoner was guilty or not guilty of murder, or they might feel that this was a case in which some amount of violence was justifiable and proper, but that the defendant went too far and, in doing so, killed a man. In that case they should return a verdict of manslaughter.

The jury took fifteen minutes to deliver their verdict: Biggin was found guilty of manslaughter. While pronouncing sentence Darling made the following remarks:

Had you been a full-grown man I should have, for this offence, although the man you killed was a citizen who could easily have been spared, passed on you a far more severe sentence than I am about to do; but you took the life of that man without justification, and as responsible for the administration of justice I

*cannot pass a less severe sentence on you than twelve months'
imprisonment with hard labour.*

Biggin bowed low with shock on hearing the judge's words
and was helped from the dock by the warders.

There is no doubt that Gregory was a sexually aggressive
man, but one can't help but feel that the verdict and sentence
were coloured as much by loathing for his homosexuality as by
any implicit condemnation of his dangerously intrusive
behaviour.

CHAPTER 12

'She Made Me Do It'

1920

If I could only see her again.

'Hendon has had a sensation this week surpassing in some respects the tragedy of July last, when Mr John Thomas Gregory was found battered to death in a wine shop at Colindale Avenue.' So began the report on the front page of the *Hendon and Finchley Times* on 7 May 1920.

Few of the killers depicted in this book will excite the same degree of contempt in the reader as does Arthur Andrew Clement Goslett. For, whereas momentary rage, mental illness or desperate need, serve to fuel most of the killings depicted in these pages, in Goslett's case we see nothing more then pure lust and selfishness as motives. Likewise, we have seen (and will see) many murderers confess to their crime out of conscience or simple lack of the criminal mentality. However, Goslett tried with everything in his power to deny any responsibility, either for his actions, or – when all else failed – the inevitable consequence of these, courtesy of the hangman's noose.

The River Brent flows through the lowest, south-west part of the old Borough of Hendon, amidst what was still, in the 1920s, a swampy, sparsely populated area. There was, as yet, no North Circular Road running alongside the river, and no Northern Line railway crossing the stream by viaduct en route to Edgware – both would arrive in the next five years or so. There *was* building work taking place, though, as the London suburbs continued their inexorable encroachment on the remains of rural Middlesex. The houses in Western Avenue, today a quiet street running down from behind Brent Cross underground station to the North Circular Road, were as yet only half-built. Brentmead Place, a row of small houses running parallel with the river, had been completed only recently. There were also allotments along the floor of the valley and it was one of the users of these, a Mr Mosley, who summoned the police on the morning of Sunday, 2 May 1920. Within a short while Dr Holgate Shaw, the police surgeon for S Division, joined Sergeant Burgess and PC Wheedon, who had answered the call. For what Mr Mosley had found was the body of a middle-aged woman resting in the shallow water of the Brent.

The dead woman was lying on her back with her head facing downstream. She was dressed in a brown skirt and a grey jumper. Any suggestion that her death was the result of suicide or of an accident was dispelled by the large patches of blood visible on dry land some yards from where the copse was found, which suggested that she had been thrown into the stream after being attacked. The body was removed from the water and placed on the bank to enable Dr Shaw to examine it more closely. The woman's hair was matted with blood, which had come from four deep wounds in the back of the head. Dr Shaw concluded that she had died about twelve hours previously.

The River Brent, c 1920. LBB

The suspicion that a murder had been committed brought Detective Inspectors Miles and Duggan of S Division to the site, and they were followed shortly afterwards by Chief Detective Inspector Neil from Scotland Yard.

A search of the body revealed a tradesman's receipt marked with the woman's details: her name was Evelyn Goslett, and she lived in Armitage Mansions, a group of flats situated above shops on Golders Green Road, about a mile distant. A check showed that Evelyn Goslett had already been reported as missing: at about ten that morning Jules, her eldest son, had informed the police at Golders Green of her absence over the previous night. An officer, who also happened to be a friend of the Gosletts, had dropped by at Armitage Mansions. He informed Chief Detective Inspector Neil that the deceased's husband, Arthur Goslett, had still been in bed at 11.00 am and had shown little concern for his missing wife.

Chief Detective Inspector Neil, Inspector Duggan and Sergeant Burgess called at the address that afternoon inquiring after Evelyn Goslett's husband. When he came to the door – wearing a smart striped suit – the policemen asked to speak to him in private. Duggan stated later, in court, that he'd had 'a certain suspicion' about Goslett as soon as he met him. This 'suspicion' must have been intensified by Goslett's

Golders Green Road, c.1920. LBB

reaction to what would, in the normal run of things, be taken as shocking news: 'I am making enquiries touching upon the death of your wife, Evelyn Goslett...' Neil announced – to which Goslett had responded with a curiously matter-of-fact 'Yes' – '...whose body was found in the River Brent today.' Goslett was promptly cautioned, illustrating the incredulity of the officers over his nonchalance at the news of the death of his wife, and was then asked to account for his movements on the previous evening.

Goslett claimed he had spent the afternoon and evening in Richmond, where he had visited a public house and wandered along the bank of the Thames. He had arrived home at about 10.30 and, noticing his wife's absence, had asked after her before retiring to bed. Something in his manner led the police to believe he was lying.

Mrs Goslett was the daughter of a well-known local businesswoman, Mrs Binko, who ran an agency hiring parlour maids. Described as a charming woman, she had three children – all teenagers in 1920 – from her previous marriage, which had ended with the death of her husband. She also had a two-year-old daughter, Leonie, from her current marriage.

She had been seen in Mr Ben Jones' shop in Golders Green road at about 8.00 pm on Saturday evening. The manager, Alfred Murray, told the police she had seemed perfectly happy. She had told him, 'Pa is taking me to see a new house. We are going to put a down payment on it this evening.'

Her husband, Arthur Goslett, aged forty-three, was an unusual man. Born in South Africa of wealthy parents, he had spent his early youth in the firm of which his father was the head. Later he fell out with his family and decided to come to England. He married Evelyn in 1914 and lived with her, Leonie and Jules at the flat in Golders Green Road. He had served in the Royal Navy during the recent hostilities, in which he had been engaged in building and repairing aeroplanes at the aircraft works in Cricklewood and Kingsbury. At one point he had been closely watched by secret service officials who had suspected him of being a spy. Nothing came of it, however, and, after being demobbed, he obtained work at a furniture manufactory. He often walked about wearing the uniform of a naval lieutenant, was a heavy drinker, favouring whisky, and was also fatally drawn to the charms of the opposite sex.

Chief Detective Inspector Neil and Sergeant Burgess searched Goslett's bedroom. They found a small brooch which Mrs Goslett was fond of, and had been seen wearing on Saturday afternoon. This strengthened their suspicion that Goslett had been in the company of his wife that evening. Goslett was taken to Golders Green Police Station for further questioning. Here he made two statements reiterating his claim that he had been in Richmond on Saturday afternoon and evening.

The police also interviewed the other occupants of the flat: these included Mrs Goslett's children, a pretty twenty-seven-year-old shop assistant named Daisy Holt, and a married couple, Marjorie and Albert Orrell. According to Mrs Orrell, she had been alone with Daisy Holt all Saturday evening. At about 9.40 they had heard the front door bang and somebody had gone upstairs into the Goslett's bedroom. Later, Jules had returned home and reported finding the front door wide open, which was unusual. Understandably concerned about intruders, Mrs Orrell, Daisy Holt and Jules had searched the house but found nobody there. At about 10.40 Mr Goslett had come in. He had been wearing his naval uniform. This had been found slung over a chair when the bedroom was being searched, and it was noted that the trousers were damp up to the knee. Mrs Orrell said that the striped suit he had on when the police arrived was one she had never seen him wear before.

Mr Orrell told the police of a conversation he'd had with Goslett in the dining room at about 11.30 on Saturday evening. They had talked of general things and then Goslett had retired. The next morning Goslet told Mr Orrell that his wife had not returned home: 'Look here, old man,' Goslett had said, 'what is the good of me getting up and pacing about London looking for my wife? If she is out of town she will not be back so early on account of the Sunday trains.' It was shortly after this that Jules had reported his mother missing. Mr Orrell also stated that at about 11 am on Sunday he had seen Goslett sitting in an armchair crying 'If I could only see her again.'

As if this weren't bad enough, Daisy Holt revealed that Goslett had bigamously married her in February 1919 in a civil ceremony. He had eventually confessed his already-married status to her, and threatened to shoot her unless she moved in with him and Mrs Goslett under the guise of being his dead brother's widow. Mrs Goslett had soon discovered the true nature of their relationship and had understandably felt aggrieved. A week or so before the murder Goslett had told Mr Orrell that 'They want to clear Daisy Holt out. You will see something strange happen here.'

More importantly, Daisy Holt was pregnant as a result of a night spent with Goslett in February, while Mrs Goslett had been away on a break. The police reasoned that the stresses resulting from this situation may have provided Goslett with a motive for murdering his wife. Goslett was subsequently charged with the offence of bigamy, this providing the police with grounds for keeping him in custody and subjecting him to closer questioning. Daisy Holt was to play an important part in the subsequent trial, during which Goslett sought with every means at his disposal to depict her as the agent of his – and Mrs Goslett's – misfortunes.

If the investigating officers thought that Goslett would continue to deny any involvement in the murder of his wife they were wrong: on the Tuesday evening he cracked and, over the next two days, made no less than six further statements in which he confessed, giving varying accounts of the same event in each. Immediately after the first confession he was charged with murder. The prosecution would finally rest on one of the statements in particular. In this he admitted to the murder but alleged that he did it at the instigation of Daisy Holt, whilst he was under the influence of drink:

This affair is all through her. She alienated my affection from my wife, and she has been the instigation of this murder. I am going to have the rope, and am going down under. I am speaking the truth, believe me, inspector. I have been putting it off from day to day for the last six months. I meant doing it a couple of nights before but my heart failed me.

The Prince Albert, *Golders Green c.1922.* LBB

Witness statements verified that the husband and wife had gone out together on the Thursday evening to look at a house. Referring to this earlier, baulked opportunity to murder his wife, Goslett described how he'd had to face Daisy Holt's wrath as a result: 'She called me a coward when I saw her afterwards, the same as she has often done. I killed the best woman. I see my mistake. She is the coward.'

Goslett then went on to describe the lead-up to the murder. The plan had been to lure Mrs Goslett down to the banks of the Brent under the pretence of looking at one of the new houses being built on Western Avenue. He arranged to meet his wife at 9.15, at the *Prince Albert* public house, near Brent Bridge, and together they would go and view the new property:

> *On Saturday, May 1, at 7am, I told my wife to meet me at an hotel at nine-fifteen that night to look at a house. When I left home at four o'clock to go to Richmond I put a tyre lever in my pocket. I took it with me for the purpose of killing my wife that night.*

A search of the flat would uncover the tyre lever, hidden in a cupboard: when it was shown to Goslett he said: 'This is the

one, Sir. Believe me: this is the one.' At the same time a
handbag containing jewellery was found. This, the Orrells
assured the police, Mrs Goslett usually carried with her. Inside
the bag was a purse stained with blood.

After meeting at the *Prince Albert*, the husband and wife had
threaded through to Western Avenue where the 'new house'
was situated. Heading down this road into the valley of the
River Brent, they had approached the stream. Goslett goes on
to describe the killing of Evelyn Goslett in graphic detail:

> *As we were walking along she said: 'It is rather a long way.' I did
> not know there was a river there until I came up to it. It was the
> other woman who suggested I should take my wife down there to
> that place and stun her and throw her into the river…. I struck
> her on the back of the head with the tyre lever. I struck her three
> or four blows. She was clean gone when she fell. I kissed her
> goodbye, took the ring from her finger and away she went. When
> she fell I took the jewellery from her neck, the pendent and chain,
> and the ear-rings from her ears.*

Goslett finished the statement and then, perhaps relieved at
having 'let it out' he asked for the pen once more and wrote
'this is King's evidence I am giving here' at the bottom of the
page. King's evidence (nowadays, Queen's evidence) was
evidence or information given by one defendant against
another, often in return for a discounted sentence or pardon.
It is probable that Goslett did not know the exact meaning of
the phrase. Nevertheless, this addendum was to have
interesting implications during the eventual trial.

Goslett had been seen in Richmond on Saturday evening.
However, inquiries showed that it would have been possible
for him to travel from that place to Brondesbury (in Kilburn)
by train and make his way to the *Prince Albert* in time to meet
Mrs Goslett.

The inquest opened at Hendon Town Hall on Wednesday 5
May. There was a large crowd in attendance, hoping to catch
a glimpse of the accused. In this they were disappointed.
Goslett, firmly ensconced in Brixton Prison, had been given
the opportunity to attend but declined the offer.

The coroner, Dr George Cohen, announced that his intention was merely to take formal evidence at this stage in the proceedings from the mother of the victim and from the doctors, one of whom was Bernard Spilsbury.

Mrs Binko verified the identity of the victim and then asked if she might say 'a word.' Cohen told her that he preferred her not to do so at this point, but that she would later have an opportunity to say what she liked.

Dr Holgate Shaw gave his evidence, pointing out that Mrs Goslett had died as a result of drowning and not from the wounds to her head. Dr Spilsbury, who had carried out the post-mortem, verified the previous doctor's evidence for the main part, merely adding that he'd noticed a small bruise on the right hand of the murdered woman.

The coroner's officer, PC Leeds then presented Goslett's trousers and boots to the court. 'I want you to feel the bottom of these trousers' Cohen told the jury, 'You will feel that they are damp up to a certain point. We shall refer to this at the next hearing, and now I just want you to note the dampness.' With that, the hearing was adjourned until 18 May.

The next day Goslett appeared at Hendon Court House and was remanded to Brixton Prison for seven days. Further

Goslett leaves court. Mirrorpix

evidence was presented to the magistrates the following week, including a map of the area around the scene of crime drawn by PC William Cook. Inspector Duggan informed the court that an important witness, Daisy Holt, was in the Hendon infirmary 'undergoing an operation', and was not available to give evidence. He therefore asked for a further adjournment. This was granted and Goslett was returned to Brixton Prison.

Great interest attended Daisy Holt's appearance in the

witness box when the case was resumed on 28 May. Dressed in a neat blue dress and a black hat, she showed great self-possession when questioned by Sir Richard Muir, representing the Crown. Daisy Holt told the court that she had met Goslett in late 1918 and had married him at a registry office in White Hart Lane, Tottenham, in February 1919. At that time she had believed his family name to be Godfrey. They had briefly lived together in Forest Road, Kew. Goslett had frequently been absent at the weekends, flying planes to Dunkirk on behalf of the War Ministry – or so he had assured her. In May, when she went into hospital for a termination on health grounds, Goslett visited her, and it was then that he told her that he was already married.

After hearing all the evidence the magistrates remanded Goslett to appear at the Old Bailey on the capital charge. As he was led below Goslett lost his temper, shouting to the court, 'It was her! She made me do it!' The two prison officers in attendance restrained him and he was manhandled into the cells.

On 2 June the inquest was resumed, the jury concluding that Evelyn Goslett had been murdered by Arthur Goslett. Her body released, Mrs Goslett was buried in the Jewish cemetery at Hoop Lane, Golders Green.

Goslett's trial opened at the Old Bailey on 21 June before Mr Justice Shearman. The defending counsel was Mr Henry Curtis Bennett KC, who was later to defend Edith Thompson in the infamous Thompson-Bywaters murder trial in 1922. Mr Eustace Fulton handled the case for the prosecution.

Curtis Bennett asked for the newly sworn-in jury to be made absent while he challenged the prosecution's intention to use one of the statements Goslett had made as evidence. This concerned the statement in which Goslett had written 'This is King's evidence that I am giving here.' Curtis Bennett argued that Goslett had made this particular statement under the impression that he was going to be used as King's evidence against some other party. Justice Shearman disagreed, expressing the view that the statement was voluntary and that it could be used by the prosecution. However, he did grant Curtis Bennett permission to cross-examine the police before the statement was presented in court.

Notwithstanding the plea of 'not guilty' submitted by Goslett, the defence's hope was to secure a verdict of manslaughter on their client's behalf. That Goslett had killed his wife was hardly in doubt; the question was rather one of *in what state of mind* had the defendant been at the time of the murder.

A large number of witnesses were called for the prosecution. These included Daisy Holt and Mrs Orrell, who had visited the accused while he was on remand. During the visit he had confessed to her that he had murdered his wife, and that he had been drunk at the time.

When Inspector Duggan entered the witness box Curtis Bennett questioned him closely on the circumstances under which the long statement made on 4 May had been made. Duggan said that the statement was begun in the presence of five officers, including Chief Detective Inspector Neil, but that they all went away with the exception of Inspector Miles and himself. Regarding the prisoner's written comment that the statement was 'King's evidence', Curtis Bennett asked: 'Nothing was said during the course of taking this statement that it would be used as King's evidence, which means it would be used against somebody else in the witness box?' to which Duggan replied: 'Nothing'.

This was clearly an important issue, because Justice Shearman now commented: 'This affects me and I must ask you some questions. Did you make him any promise of favour; did you offer to do him any good if he made a statement?' Duggan replied in the negative.

Chief Detective Inspector Neil was also cross-examined on the issue of the statement, and Justice Shearman concluded that he was satisfied the evidence was admissible: the statement was then read to the jury.

The content of the statement was clearly detrimental to the defence, amounting as it did to an admission of murder. The defence therefore shifted its emphasis and tried to show that Goslett had not been responsible for his actions at the time of the murder. A number of witnesses were called in an attempt to demonstrate this: Walter Dale, who had worked with Goslett at the Nieuport aircraft works at Cricklewood in 1916 told the jury that he had found Goslett a very curious and awkward man to deal with: 'Later, I thought he was not right in the head, and I took care to avoid him as much as possible,' he said. The witness added that he regarded Goslett as a 'crack-pot', and that when he saw the case in the paper he decided to contact the defendant's solicitor. Walter Wallace, another former co-worker of Goslett's, who had worked with him at an aircraft works at Kingsbury, said the accused had found it impossible to concentrate on his work for more than a few minutes at a time. He had also complained frequently of headaches. According to Wallace, Goslett had been known amongst the staff as 'the mad skipper'.

Dr Frederick Toogood, called as a medical expert by the defence, said that Goslett had told him he had been in a serious plane accident in Germany in 1913, in which he had been knocked unconscious for a day and a half. The witness said he had found marks on Goslett's head consistent with this story and that if, as Goslett had told him, he had consumed twenty drinks on the night of the murder, he would certainly be unfit to judge the nature and quality of any act he had committed. 'Do you mean he would not know whether he was hitting his wife or a tree?' Justice Shearman asked, to which Dr Toogood replied in the affirmative.

Cross-examined by the prosecution, Dr Toogood said that he had found Goslett to be under a 'dominating influence.' He had repeated several times, 'She made me do it' – referring presumably to Daisy Holt – and had asked: 'You don't think I shall dangle, shall I? I would like to see *her* dangle.' Dr Toogood admitted that there was not a lot of alcohol in twenty drinks 'nowadays' but insisted that even a small amount of drink would adversely affect a man with head injuries such as those suffered by Goslett.

Dr Griffiths, the chief Medical officer at Brixton said that he had never seen any indication of insanity during his many interviews with Goslett.

Curtis Bennett's final speech lasted over an hour: he submitted that, apart from the so-called confessions, there was not a scrap of evidence on which they could convict Goslett. The statements themselves were full of contradictory, almost hallucinatory material. Goslett had felt he was being compelled by some irresistible force to kill his wife and was suffering under an insane delusion. What sane man would think it was a defence in law to claim that a woman forced him to commit murder?

Fulton's reply took forty minutes. He pointed out that Goslett's conduct was the result of the situation he found himself in, with two women and two families to support, and that, while what he did was undoubtedly wrong, it was also perfectly intelligible and, in that sense, sane.

Justice Shearman then summed up, advising the jury that they were not to consider whether Goslett was eccentric or abnormal, but simply whether he was mad. The jury retired to consider their verdict. Eight minutes later they returned: Goslett was found guilty. As the death sentence was announced the prisoner merely raised his eyebrows a little and was then led below.

Goslett remained unrepentant to the end. A few days before his execution he told a friend, who visited him in prison, that he felt it unreasonable that he should hang for something for which he was not solely responsible. He attributed his present situation simply to the fact that he had thought too much of women. Because of this, Goslett felt he would not hang. Such arguments could never have saved Goslett's life. However, an attempt was made to win a retrial, on the basis of the supposed wrongful admission of evidence and misdirection of the jury by the judge. This was unsuccessful and Goslett was hanged at Pentonville Prison by John Ellis and Edward Taylor on 27 July.

CHAPTER 13

He Tried to Disappear

1930

He slid down, his hat falling off. I saw he had a
bald patch on the back of his head.

This murder took place far from Barnet, in the village of Hardingstone in Northamptonshire, but it has been included here because the killer lived in Finchley. Further, the victim – an unemployed itinerant – was 'hired' solely to fulfil the murderer's purposes during a chance meeting in Whetstone High Road. The case has aroused considerable interest through the years, partly because the victim has never been identified, and also because during the trial the prosecution relied on scientific evidence to a previously unprecedented degree.

In late 1930 Alfred Arthur Rouse was apparently doing well for himself. The thirty-six-year-old commercial traveller for a firm of braces and garter manufacturers was the owner of a small semi-detached house in Buxted Road, midway between North Finchley and Friern Barnet. Here he lived with his wife, Lily May, and their supposedly adopted child. Good looking and ostensibly carefree, Rouse's career took him the length and breadth of Britain in his little Morris Minor. Yet beneath the calm domestic surface Rouse was a worried man. Utilising his flair for chat, Rouse took advantage of the opportunities his job gave him to bed dozens of women. As a result his life was in shreds; in October 1930 a maid based in Hendon, Nellie Tucker, gave birth to her second child by Rouse (the first was, in fact, the child living with Rouse and his wife). And, as if to top that, a further woman, Ivy Jenkins of Glamorgan, was bearing another of his babies, due at any moment. These unfortunate circumstances were merely the latest in a long line of romantic mishaps for Rouse. A string of maintenance orders was pushing him steadily into debt: he'd had enough and decided that drastic action was necessary to release him from the chaos of his affairs. What better way out than to 'die' and begin life anew elsewhere?

It was the early hours of the 6 November 1930 – a morning still lit by the glare of numerous Guy Fawkes' bonfires. Two young men, Alfred Brown and William Bailey, were returning from a firework display in Northampton. As they walked along Hardingstone Lane at about 2 am they saw a man emerge from a roadside ditch. At the same moment they noticed a fire blazing half-a-mile or so down the road. 'It looks as if somebody is burning a fire' the man said and then set off at a pace towards the main London-Northampton road. They were later to describe him to the police as of stocky build, and they noted he was carrying a small suitcase.

At first the two men assumed it was a bonfire blazing away down the road. However, they were in for a surprise; turning a corner they were greeted by the sight of a car burning in the middle of the road. They ran to the village to get help and returned with two local constables. After putting the fire out the four men were presented with the ghastly sight of a badly burnt body slumped in the wreck. A police investigation began in order to determine what had happened.

Fortunately the car's rear number plate, MU 1468, had survived the fire. This enabled the police to quickly trace the car to A A Rouse of Buxted Road, Finchley. Mrs Rouse was taken to Northampton to identify what were presumed to be the remains of her husband, but this, of course, she could not do.

A search of the ground around the wreck had uncovered a mallet in some bushes nearby. The police linked the description of the man from the roadside ditch to that of her husband given by Mrs Rouse. The suspicion grew that a murder had occurred, and Rouse's description was circulated to the press.

The afternoon after the fire a Miss Phyllis Jenkins, of Gellygaer, Glamorgan, bought a copy of the *Daily Sketch* containing a description of the incident. She showed it to her sister Ivy's *amour*, Arthur Rouse, who had unexpectedly arrived earlier that day complaining that his car had been stolen *en route*. Phyllis asked Rouse if it was his car, but he denied it. However, the next day the *Daily Sketch* carried more details, including Rouse's name. His cover blown, Rouse boarded a bus for London on the evening of 7 November. The suspicious Phyllis informed Scotland Yard and, when he got off the bus at Victoria Station, Rouse was met by Detective Sergeant Skelly and taken to Hammersmith Police Station. Here he was subjected to a relentless all-night grilling, during which a statement was taken as to how and why the fatal fire had occurred.

Rouse told the police that he had been travelling overnight to Leicester and had picked up a hitchhiker. He tried to claim initially that his passenger had stolen the car, but then he changed his story. He had taken a wrong turn, he said, and found himself in Hardingstone Lane. At that point he decided to stop for a nap. According to his statement he had got out of the car to relieve himself and asked his passenger to fill the petrol tank with the contents of a can kept on the back seat. The man had then, according to Rouse, asked him if he had something he could smoke. Rouse, a non-smoker, conveniently had a cigar in his bag and had given it to the man.

Rouse went on to say that he had left the car and walked over 200 yards to relieve himself. On his way back he saw the car burst into flames. He said he tried to reach the man trapped in the car but had failed and panicked.

Understandably unconvinced by Rouse's account, the police started to look into the background of this man and found out some interesting facts. He had been born on 6 April 1894, in Herne Hill, South London. Following his wedding in November 1914 he had left to serve in France in the Great War. It was while on service in May 1915 that he had received a head wound. This may have accounted for Rouse's compulsive womanising: certain types of brain injury can result in increased libidinal activity, and it is possible that Rouse's injury was of this type. Inspector Lawrence, one of the interviewing detectives, later told the police court at Northampton that Rouse persistently bragged of his sexual conquests.

When he left the army he got a job as a travelling salesman, his job taking him over a wide area. This had given him the opportunity to woo his way into the lives and beds of dozens of women. His business diary contained a 'visiting list' of over eighty women he saw routinely on his travels and, by 1930, this had resulted in several illegitimate children and bigamous marriages. These facts provided the police with a motive, and Rouse was charged with murder. After three appearances at Northampton police court he was committed for trial.

The trial opened on 26 January 1931 at Northampton Assizes before an all-male jury. This was at the insistence of the defence, who had expressed concern at the prospect of outraged womanhood distorting the jury's ruminations. Rouse was defended by D L Finnemore, the barrister who had represented him at the prolonged police court proceedings. Mr Norman Birkett K C – later to be one of the judges at Nuremberg – acted for the Crown, and the judge was Mr Justice Talbot. The national press had picked up the case and as a result the so-called 'Blazing Car Murder Trial' made daily headlines for its duration.

The long-suffering Mrs Rouse attended, dressed, according to the *Hendon and Finchley Times,* in 'an apple-green hat, from beneath which peeped her auburn hair; a dark coat with a fur collar; and a light brown dress.' The same reporter described the accused as: 'A handsome man. He is dark and well built and wears a small moustache.' He wore a well-tailored suit throughout, along with a brown silk tie and spats. On trial for his life, Rouse suffered badly from nerves and his wife plied him with smelling salts and tablets during the course of the trial.

Much of the prosecution's case rested on forensic evidence provided by Dr Eric Hemingway Shaw, honorary pathologist for Northampton General Hospital. Dr Shaw was able to prove that the victim had still been alive when the car was set alight. This view was supported by the testimony of Sir Bernard Spilsbury, who pointed out that black deposits in the victim's air passages indicated that he was alive and continued to breathe for sometime after the fire started. While this did not conflict with Rouse's claim that the fire was an accident, Spilsbury had also identified serious injuries to the victim's skull. Even worse, Shaw stated that fragments of cloth taken from the dead man's trousers had been soaked in petrol.

But most damning of all was the evidence gleaned from the mallet found in some bushes close to the wreck of the car. Two sets of hairs were found on the mallet – long brown hairs and short dark hairs. It was shown that while the first set belonged to Rouse, the others originated from the victim. This proved that Rouse had been in the same vicinity as the man, and had contact with him – a fact that he had originally denied, claiming that the car had been stolen without his knowledge.

This application of scientific principles to contribute to the conviction was groundbreaking, and is still recognized as a turning point in forensic investigation.

The jury retired to consider the evidence, taking just seventy-five minutes to return a guilty verdict. Rouse was accordingly sentenced to death. His appeal against sentence was rejected twenty-three days later and he was duly executed at Bedford prison on 10 March by Thomas William Pierrepoint, uncle of the famous hangman Albert Pierrepoint.

Shortly before the execution Rouse wrote a confession to the murder. The account is chilling in its matter-of-fact description of what took place on the night of the killing. After describing how he met his victim in a chance encounter at the *Swan and Pyramid* in Whetstone, Rouse describes how he lured the poor man into joining him on the car journey with promises of booze and the possibility of work:

> *He was the sort of man no-one would miss, and I thought he would suit the plan I had in mind. He drank the whiskey neat from the bottle and was getting quite fuzzled. We talked a lot, but he did not tell me who he actually was. I did not care.*

Rouse was similarly cold in his account of the killing:

The man was half-dozing – the effect of the whiskey. I gripped him by the throat with my right hand. I pressed his head against the back of the seat. He slid down, his hat falling off. I saw he had a bald patch on the back of his head.

Rouse then goes on to describe how he hit his victim on the head with the mallet and ignited the petrol-soaked car. Yet despite his setting the record straight with this admission, at no point does he ever express remorse for his act.

The trial of A A Rouse seems to have captured the imagination of the general public in the years since the trial. At least two books and two films based on the case have appeared. In Alan Moore's cult novel *Voice of the Fire*, set in Northampton, one chapter tells Rouse's story in first-person narrative. Rouse is depicted as a self-deceiving and arrogant man who convinces himself that he has charmed his jury into acquitting him. As we know, Moore's Rouse is in for a rude shock.

CHAPTER 14

Crack-Up

1827–1930–1944

The table downstairs was laid for breakfast.

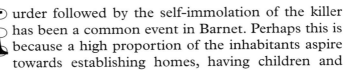

urder followed by the self-immolation of the killer has been a common event in Barnet. Perhaps this is because a high proportion of the inhabitants aspire towards establishing homes, having children and generally attempting to put down roots and live the decent life. When it goes wrong, as unfortunately it frequently does, there is likely to be an overwhelming sensation of one's 'world falling apart'. In extreme cases despair gives way to a moment's madness and, with the foul deed done, suicide follows as the inevitable next step. Certainly, many of our killings seem to arise out of domestic difficulties, and the pressures generated by broken relations or human frailty, rather than through simple brutishness. In this chapter I present a set of murders, each occurring within an apparently normal domestic setting, each followed by the killer's own suicide, either actual or attempted.

The Times, for 3 and 4 August 1827 gives an account on the murder in Hadley of a Mrs Mary Spencer, widow, by her daughter – also named Mary Spencer – who then cut her own throat. The mother was about eighty years old, the daughter nearly fifty.

For the previous twenty years the pair had lived together in reasonable circumstances following the death some time before of Mr Spencer, who had kept livery stables. The daughter, from all accounts, was devoted to her mother's every need. Lately, though, things seem to have gone increasingly awry. Both suffered from what is described in *The Times* as 'nervous complaints', and fell back on a diet of watery gruel in the belief that this would benefit their condition, despite the protestations of their medical practitioner. More recently the daughter had begun to act strangely, so much so that Mrs Spencer had grown apprehensive and had asked one of the servants to sleep in her room with her to keep an eye on things.

The daughter was particularly distraught about the failure of her sister's marriage. Her brother-in-law's business had collapsed leaving the sister and her family in what *The Times* describes as 'a state of some embarrassment'. Mary Spencer junior had begged her mother to help the sister out financially and in the way of some pieces of furniture but the old lady had resolutely refused to do this. These circumstances had exacerbated the younger Mary Spencer's anxiety enormously.

On the morning of Tuesday, 1 August the servants of the house found the bodies of mother and daughter upstairs, in the bedroom. Their throats had been cut, and they were completely saturated in blood. A bloody razor, later identified as one used by Mrs Spencer to cut corns from her feet, was found near the spot. The following day an inquest was opened at the *White Bear* public house, Hadley, before the coroner, Thomas Stirling. After the swearing in of the jury the inquest was adjourned to the drawing room of Mrs Spencer's house. Here the jury was greeted with the sight of the still-bloody victims of the tragedy.

The first witness was Dr Walter Morrison of Barnet, who had been called to the house the previous morning in response to the gruesome discovery. He testified that the Spencers had already been dead several hours at that point and that death in both cases was the result of injuries to the throat. In order to illustrate his conclusion, Dr Morrison obligingly washed the bodies under the gaze of the jury, in order to display the extent of the wounds. Dr William Hammond of Whetstone corroborated the evidence given previously, adding that in the younger woman's case the injuries were less severe, and that her death must therefore have been lingeringly painful

Ann White, the cook, described how the previous night everything had appeared to be normal. About eight o'clock on the Tuesday, the ladies not having come down for breakfast, a housemaid called for them. Receiving no reply the maid and cook made their way upstairs and, upon entering the bedchamber, found the beds both spattered with a great quantity of blood.

A nurse of the family told the inquest that Miss Spencer had been very disturbed of late and had seemed on occasion 'out of her senses.' Other witnesses verified this. After the coroner's summing up the jury retired for a few moments before returning the verdict: 'That Mary Spencer, senior, met her death from wounds inflicted by her daughter, who afterwards cut her own throat, being at that time in a state of mental derangement.' Immediately after the inquest the bodies were placed in leaden coffins. The internment, from all accounts, was a private affair.

We move forward over a hundred years now, to Edgware in 1930. Recent years had seen a vast growth in the population of the former village on Watling Street, a growth stimulated more by the building of the Watford By-pass than by the

Penshurst Gardens, Edgware, 2007. The author

extension of the Charing Cross tube from Golders Green in 1924. A suburb known as New Edgware began to spread out from the village's main thoroughfare, eating its way through the old fields in the direction of the Hale. These were fine houses, each with its own garden and garage. Shops appeared in larger numbers around the railway station. For a businessman working in London all week the attractions of life in Edgware must have been great.

The notion of violence, repressed or real, lurking behind the net curtains of suburban life is a commonplace nowadays. Perhaps at some level we even take a perverse delight in witnessing the unravelling of somebody else's attempt to create a decent life. In the Edgware of 1930 the events described below must have been truly unnerving.

Concerns had been growing for some time for the mental health of William Clarence Tuke, a chartered accountant living at Marcroft, a detached house in Penshurst Gardens, Edgware. Hard work and devotion to his family had enabled Tuke to establish a fine home in this quiet suburban street and here he lived with his wife Iva, forty-five, and son Thomas, aged fifteen, the family having moved in four years prior to the events now described. Tuke conforms to the popular idea of the 1930s incorporated accountant: he was a short man with a heavy black moustache, much given to wearing dark suits. He was a stalwart in the community and had been treasurer of the local branch of the League of Nations Union. In 1929 Tuke resigned from the post, complaining of overwork. The secretary described him as 'a jolly and good-hearted man. He was an enthusiastic tennis player, and he and his wife were members of one of the local tennis clubs.'

Doctor Moriarty, a resident of Edgware, was particularly worried about his friend. The doctor had been treating his fellow golf club member for 'nerve problems' these last few weeks. On the morning of Wednesday, 26 March he received a phone call from a mutual friend, a Mrs Semken. She informed Moriarty that Tuke had not turned up for work for two days. Worried, Moriarty decided to visit the Tukes' house, arriving just before noon. He noted with some concern that the curtains were drawn and the milk bottles still stood on the doorstep. Full of misgivings, he alerted the police.

A phone call brought two officers from Edgware Police Station, Sergeant Price and PC Wixen. Price forced entry to the house through the kitchen window and let the other two in through the front door.

Doctor Moriarty's fear that things were amiss was confirmed when, upon entering the house, the group of men spotted a trail of blood leading across the floor to the door into the garage. Entering they saw Tuke's Essex saloon car standing with its door open and somebody lying on the car's floor covered in a blanket. A groan indicated that the man was still alive and, peeling the blanket aside, Moriarty recognised the figure as that of his friend. His throat had been torn open and a large quantity of blood covered his hands and the carpet on the floor of the car.

Sergeant Price acted quickly, summoning an ambulance and upon its arrival Wixen accompanied the unfortunate Tuke to the Redhill Hospital (today the Edgware Community Hospital) close by, where the injured man was given emergency surgery.

One can well imagine the horror of such a scene but for Moriarty and Price worse was yet to come. Climbing the staircase to the first floor they found a bloody hammer lying on the carpet by the open doorway to a bedroom. Inside, lying on his bed, was Tuke's fifteen-year-old son. His head was coated with blood and there were splashes of this on the wall and ceiling. He was wearing pyjamas and was covered with a quilt, suggesting he had been attacked while asleep.

Next door they found Tuke's wife, also still in bed. Her head was concealed by a pillow, the removal of which revealed a thick pool of blood spread over her badly bruised face. The briefest of examinations was all Moriarty needed to pronounce both mother and son dead.

It was found also that the bath was two-thirds full of bloody water. On the floor lay an open bloodstained razor. Yet amidst all this horror it was noted that the kitchen table was laid neatly for breakfast. What had happened in this otherwise normal suburban house to create such a meteoric scene of destruction? The police opened a murder inquiry.

Naturally, the officers of the law were eager to speak to William Tuke as soon as this became possible. As noted above, Tuke had been rushed to surgery as soon as he'd arrived at hospital. His windpipe had been completely severed by a razor or a knife and he was lucky to survive the injury. Whether he felt that way two days later is conjecture, for he was visited at his bedside by Divisional Detective Inspector Bennett and Detective Inspector Andrews of S Division.

According to police reports Tuke was staggered to hear his wife and son were dead, his response to the news being a shocked 'I know nothing about this'. By now the police were certain that Tuke had killed his family and yet he professed to recall nothing of the events of the day of the killing. Was this claim genuine or merely a simple case of a murderer trying to slip the net of justice?

Further inquiries revealed that Tuke had a history of blackouts. As far back as 1920 he had been brought home by a man who had found him wandering around South Mimms in a daze. The next morning he'd had a vacant look in his eyes and complained of his head hurting. He had been unable to offer any explanation as to how he'd ended up in such a situation. While this may indicate the possibility of alcoholic intoxication, Tuke, from all accounts was a near teetotaller. In 1923 he'd had a breakdown and had recuperated in Jersey. In 1929, he'd again hovered close to breakdown, on this occasion induced by overwork, and his family had urged him to 'ease up', this time successfully.

The police questioned Tuke's managing clerk, Dorothy Didham, who'd worked with him for twelve years. She had visited the Tukes on the day before the killing, 25 March, to find out why he hadn't come into work that day, and was the last person – excluding Tuke himself -who had seen the victims alive. She recalled that Tuke had driven her to Edgware station at about 10.15 pm. Mrs Tuke and the boy had been preparing to go to bed. Didham told the police that Tuke had seemed very worried about business affairs. When Tuke failed to turn up for work the next day she'd phoned her friend Mrs Semken, who'd contacted Moriarty.

The Tukes' neighbour, Teresa Smiles, made two statements to the police in which she described a visit to the Tuke household two weeks before the discovery of the bodies. On that occasion she was left for a period in the lounge with

William Tuke and was disturbed to find her formerly friendly neighbour uncommunicative. He spent the duration of her visit staring into space, and over the next two hours Tuke hardly spoke at all. Mrs Smiles was left feeling understandably uncomfortable and asked Mrs Tuke if anything were wrong with Mr Tuke. 'Mrs Tuke said "He is working far too hard, and worrying far too much, and if he goes on like this much longer he will have another breakdown and then I don't know what will happen".' 'These weren't the exact words but it was something to that effect,' she added.

Shortly afterwards Tuke, a pathetic figure with a heavily bandaged throat, appeared at the Hendon Petty Sessions. Among the onlookers in the packed courtroom were his brother, the Reverend Walter Sidney Tuke from Rochdale, and Iva Tuke's brother James Stansfield. Mr E Clayton appeared for the prosecution; Mr F H Plummer represented Tuke. He pleaded not guilty to both charges of murder.

Walter Tuke gave evidence, claiming that his nephew was mentally backward and that this had worried the accused, causing him to become highly strung. When Tuke had been studying in London in 1906 the door to his room had had to be forced open and he had been found suffering from a sort of trance. He had also had a serious breakdown in 1913.

Hilda Merrick, formerly employed as a cook at Marcroft, identified the hammer found at the scene as one that she'd seen kept on a bench in the garage.

Dr R M Bronte, who'd carried out the post-mortem on the bodies, said that Mrs Tuke had suffered seven head wounds. Her skull was shattered to pieces on the left-hand side. The boy had four wounds and there was extensive fracturing of the skull. He added that the blows must have been of extreme violence and could have been delivered with the hammer presented in court.

Dr Moriarty, Dorothy Didham and Police Sergeant Price gave further evidence verifying their respective statements. Dr Hosford described Tuke's condition upon his admission to the Redhill Hospital and was of the opinion that the wound to his throat was self-inflicted. He reiterated what he'd said at the inquest, that Tuke, upon coming round from his injuries had exhibited no prior knowledge of the deaths of his wife and son.

Tuke was committed for trial at the Central Criminal Court. Mr Plummer then said that he wished to thank the police for the courtesy and tactfulness with which they had handled the case.

When the case came to trial Tuke was quickly declared unfit to plea and was placed for an indefinite period in a secure hospital for the criminally insane.

A few days later *The Times* published a letter from Tuke's brother in which he once again expressed his gratitude for the courtesy with which his brother had been treated:

> *I cannot resist a desire to make public my admiration for the London Police. The Edgware tragedy, which brought my brother for trial on the capital charge this week at the Old Bailey has necessarily brought myself and others into proximity with the police. I have had rare opportunities therefore of observing from the inside, some of the methods of the police force, sometimes adversely criticised, and I am filled with admiration and gratitude for the unfailing courtesy and kindly consideration shown by Scotland Yard inspectors, Edgware police officers and prison officials of every rank towards their prisoner and his friends.*
>
> *I shall always remember that the darkest period of my brother's life and of my own was considerably lightened from the last quarter from which I expected it.*

The final case examined here occurs in the last winter of the Second World War. Robert Vernon Hart, seventy-two, was a well known and successful local builder. His company had constructed many of the houses in Golders Green, including the one he shared with his wife Muriel, sixty-two, in Ravenscroft Gardens. The couple had lived at their address for over twenty years and were a popular couple. In recent years Mr Hart's sons had joined the business and many of the houses in Winnington Road, in the Hampstead Garden Suburb had also been designed and constructed by Robert Hart and Sons Ltd.

Ravenscroft Gardens, 2008. The author

At 11 o'clock on the morning of Sunday, 10 December 1944 the housekeeper, Grace Russell, arrived for work as usual. She proceeded to go about her routine work, despite the house being silent – this was in keeping with the Harts' Sunday morning routine; they often rose to cook breakfast and prepare lunch and then stayed in bed until noon.

At first everything seemed as normal; the Sunday roast was cooking slowly in the oven, the table was laid. However, upon going upstairs to the first floor to collect the teapot and cups left over from the Harts' habitual breakfast in bed, the housekeeper was horrified to find Mrs Hart lying with her arms outstretched on the floor of the small bedroom. She was suffering from head injuries and nearby lay a bloodstained hammer. An open razor was also visible on the carpet, its blade coated with blood. Mr Hart was on the other side of the room. His throat had been cut but he was still breathing.

The housekeeper phoned the family doctor, Dr J R Dow, who hurried over and, upon seeing the situation immediately phoned the police. They arrived soon afterwards with the police divisional surgeon who pronounced Mrs Hart dead at the scene. A murder inquiry was begun under the direction of Detective Inspector John Smale of Golders Green Police Station.

Hendon Town Hall c.1935. LBB

An examination of the house showed that there had been no break-in and it was suspected that Mr Hart had suffered some sort of breakdown during which he had attacked his wife. Dr Dow, who had known the Harts for many years, described them as a devoted and happy couple. However, recent months had seen Mr Hart retreat into a severe depression and of late he had not left the house very often.

In the meantime Mr Hart had been taken to the Redhill Hospital where he succumbed to his injuries the following Tuesday. The same day the inquest on Mrs Hart for identification purposes was opened at Hendon Town Hall. Dr Keith Simpson, later to be Britain's first professor of forensic medicine, had performed the post-mortem and told the inquest that Mrs Hart had died from shock and haemorrhage caused by multiple injuries to the head and by throat wounds. The inquest was then adjourned.

The full inquest on the dead couple was held before a jury at the Hendon Town Hall a week later, on 19 December. After a short consultation between the members of the jury, which consisted mainly of local business men and traders, the verdict was announced: that Muriel Agnes Hart was murdered by her husband, and that Robert Vernon Hart took his own life whilst the balance of his mind was disturbed.

CHAPTER 15

The Rogues of Clay Lane

1931

Thank you, Sir. It ought to have been done twenty years ago.

It was a Monday night in early June 1931. As yet, no M1 motorway cut through the remote district of Edgwarebury, high above Edgware on the South Hertfordshire escarpment: only the railway and some sidings given over to the dumping of refuse defaced the otherwise rural air of the place. Smoke curled away from the burning rubbish tips and faded into the tall oaks lining muddy old Clay Lane half a mile away. There were flames licking at the base of the railway embankment along which trains periodically crawled before halting to deposit their load; the fire had been burning for years.

An itinerant labourer named Michael McGlade left his shack on the edge of Scratchwood and approached the flames, hoping to obtain a light for his pipe. Suddenly, McGlade stopped and stared: protruding from the smouldering refuse was the unmistakable form of a charred human arm. Glade dropped his pipe and ran off down Clay Lane to seek help.

This arrived rapidly: two police officers happened to be riding along the recently completed Watford By-pass on one of S Division's brand new motorcycle combinations. They had been enquiring into a series of burglaries at nearby Moat Mount Golf Course and were about to question some gypsies on a local encampment when McGlade hailed them. The officers dismounted and followed the tramp up the narrow old country lane. The shift from the sleek carriageways of the new arterial road, to the mud track climbing between dense hedges must have seemed like travelling back in time fifty years. Yet what these dutiful officers, fresh from their high speed dash along the bypass, were about to see was like something out of the Middle Ages.

McGlade took them to the spot, where a moment's inspection verified that the tramp had indeed been correct. One of the officers headed back down to the bypass to get support, while his colleague and McGlade sat and smoked, guarding the body.

Chief Constable Ashley, Superintendent Savage and Divisional Inspectors Bennett and Andrews, from S Division joined them shortly after. A true local 'bobby', Detective Sergeant Pickett, who was to prove a great help in the subsequent inquiry, accompanied these highly experienced officers.

Closer examination of the body, partially hidden in a stack of smouldering detritus, revealed it to be a well-built man, his head pointing towards Elstree. Part of the trunk and left forearm were burned. Upon removal of the corpse, it was found that the right forearm and both feet were burnt off. A piece of charred sackcloth had been wrapped about the head.

Clay Lane, Edgwarebury, 2007. The author

Edgwarebury Lane, 1930s. LBB

The body was taken to the mortuary at Hendon Town Hall, and the officers involved began to speculate on how the deceased had ended up in such a remote place. The initial view was that the as-yet-unnamed man was the victim of an accident. However, the possibility of foul play was kept in mind.

The following day, the eminent pathologist Sir Bernard Spilsbury examined the body. He concluded that the cause of death was fracturing of the skull and injuries to the brain. The man's jaw was also fractured, and there was a large wound to the chest. His features were beyond recognition, with the exception of traces of a sandy-coloured moustache, and, on one arm the tattoo of a red heart pierced with an arrow. Spilsbury reckoned the man to have been dead about thirty-six to forty-eight hours, and opined that the injuries resulted from repeated blows with a heavy instrument. The police now had a murder inquiry on their hands.

Detective Sergeant Pickett, who was later to be credited with possessing a 'local knowledge of the district, and persons of the class to which the dead man belonged', attended the post-mortem and expressed the view that the deceased may have originated from a number of itinerant men who slept out in huts and sheds in the vicinity of Clay Lane. In his view they were 'a quarrelsome kind' of folk.

Acting on Pickett's hunch, the police made discreet approaches towards some of the more trustworthy members of the Clay Lane tramp community and this rapidly began to pay dividends. A homeless labourer agreed to visit the mortuary to assist the police in identifying the murder victim. He recognised the body from its build and the remains of the moustache as that of a fellow tramp named Herbert Ayres, known to his friends as 'Pigsticker'. The man had been missing from his hut on Clay Lane since the previous Sunday.

Events now moved swiftly. A travelling labourer named John Armstrong contacted the police and made a statement in which he said that he had spent the previous Saturday night drinking in Edgware, and had slept at Clay Lane in a hut shared by two members of the tramp community. Their names were Oliver Newman and William Shelley, though their peers knew them as 'Tiggy' and 'Essex Moosh' respectively. Certain of the facts in Armstrong's statement concerning Newman and Shelley made it necessary for the police to arrest the two men on suspicion of murder.

Armstrong's statement gives us a compelling portrait of the two suspects:

Moosh is aged about fifty. He's five foot seven or eight. Medium build, full faced. Clean shaven with a very dark complexion. Hair, black. Black eyes. A woman is tattooed on his arm. He is dressed in striped cords, dark blue tweed jacket and waistcoat and a light trilby hat. Tiggy is about sixty. Five foot four. Thick build, round face, clean shaven, pointed nose. Hair brown with a sallow complexion. He wears a light-grey coat and light trilby hat.

A team of officers was assembled for the purpose of making the arrest, consisting of those mentioned earlier, together with a PC Seabrook. This done, the group set off to work.

Detective Inspector Bennett describes the circumstances leading up to the arrest:

Although it was dark, I accompanied the three officers [Seabrook, Pickett, and Andrews] *to the vicinity of where Moosh and Tiggy's hut was ... Sgt. Pickett knew that these men had three ferocious dogs, and so soon as any person approached within fifty yards of the hut the dogs began to bark. However, we were able, by discreet movement around the bushes surrounding this hut, to ascertain that both men were there.*

Clay Lane has not been used for many years. It is covered with thick bushes and trees on the hedges and also in the road. The grass has grown four or five feet. Knowing that these two men were desperate characters, and that one false move would raise the alarm, and therefore result in both men getting away in the darkness, or in any struggle that might ensue in effecting an arrest, I deemed it advisable to remain there with the officers until dawn.

I posted officers at various points to prevent either man escaping across the fields, and with Inspector Andrews and one or two other officers, placed myself in hiding at the entrance to Clay Lane, on the Watford By-pass.

Positioning themselves in some trees close to the by-pass, the officers waited through the night until, at 7.15 am, they saw Shelley approaching down Clay Lane. Bennett promptly stepped out from his hiding place and challenged Moosh. He said: 'I am a police officer. You answer to the description of a man named Moosh.' 'That's right' Shelley replied, Bennett then saying: 'I am making enquiries into the death of a man known to you as "Pigsticker," who was found dead at Scratchwood Sidings on Monday June 1.' Shelley's heart must have sunk as he found himself surrounded by police officers and the game clearly up. 'I don't know who you mean' he said. 'I know nothing about it.' Shelley was cautioned and removed to Edgware Police Station where Newman, who had followed down the lane a little later, eventually joined him. The Edgware Police Station, in Whitchurch Lane, was still under construction and, as a result, some of the cells were being used for administrative purposes. Nevertheless space was found for the two prisoners, who were relieved of their jackets, which were sent off for forensic examination.

The arrests having been made, the officers then took the opportunity to visit the tramps' little colony of shacks and sheds. Here they found a hefty stick – later described by

Shelley as his 'blunderbust' – which had evidently been cut from a nearby bush. It was stained with blood and, adhering to it were some hairs the colour of the dead man's moustache. Bloodstained grass was found in a hedge where it had been hurriedly thrown after being cut from the ground around the shacks. Worst of all was a large axe discovered hidden beneath the planks forming the floor of one of the dwellings. Close by was a bucket, containing bloodstained water.

When he returned to the police station, Detective Inspector Bennett was told that Oliver Newman wanted to speak to him. 'I will tell you something of what happened,' Newman said, and upon being cautioned he made a statement in which he admitted, to having murdered Herbert Ayres, aided by Shelley. According to the prisoner, neither he nor Shelley had intended to kill Ayres. A fight had broken out between the men after Shelley and Newman accused Ayres of stealing tea, sugar and bacon from their shacks. The fight had then got out of hand and – acting in self-defence – Newman had resorted to the stick in order to knock Ayres out.

Later Shelley told Pickett: 'If I could have had my way you would never have had us. I wanted to put him on the line and let the train hit him, but Tiggy would not have this. Still, he has got all he has been asking for a long time.'

At 7.20 that night Newman and Shelley were charged with the wilful murder of 'Pigsticker', to which they both replied 'I don't understand.'

The following day, Shelley and Newman appeared at the Hendon Petty Sessions. According to the newspaper reports, neither had shaved for a few days. They were described in the same item as 'shabbily dressed, of the roadster type,' the report drawing attention to the fact the two men were without their jackets. After hearing evidence from Inspector Bennett the pair were remanded in custody to appear at the same court a week later. The prisoners applied for defence fees under the Poor Prisoner's Defence Act, and this was granted.

In the meantime, the police continued to take statements from various members of the Clay Lane colony. Despite Newman's protestations concerning their lack of intention to kill Ayres, the police had managed to build up a considerable amount of evidence that suggested otherwise. They felt they now had enough to successfully prosecute Newman and Shelley for murder. The main thrust of the prosecution rested on the statement, mentioned earlier, made by John Armstrong. This contained an account of the murder as witnessed by somebody who was actually present at the time, the details of which completely undermined the story given to the police by the accused. Armstrong had stayed at Clay Lane on the night of the murder and had bedded down in Newman's shack some time before he, Shelley or Ayres had returned from Edgware. Upon retiring, Armstrong had managed to doze off, but was wakened by the sound of raised voices outside the shack. Shortly afterwards he heard a number of loud thuds, and a man kept shouting, 'Oh dear.' The voice was that of Ayres. Looking out into the moonlit lane Armstrong saw the forms of two men whom he recognised as Newman and Shelley was striking Ayres with the 'blunderbust'. After that things had been quiet for about twenty minutes. Hearing another series of thuds, Armstrong had peered out of the shack again and saw an axe being dropped into a pail of water and the two tramps lifting what looked like a body before carrying it off in the direction of the railway sidings.

Understandably, John Armstrong had been terrified and he resolved to make himself scarce at the first opportunity. He lay quite still lest the two killers became aware he had witnessed the murder, and early the next morning made his excuses before packing his things and leaving. As he was setting off Shelley had approached him and said: 'Geordie, if anyone asks you about Pigsticker...' to which he replied, 'Yes I know all about it. Mum's the word.' But after reading a report of the murder in the press, he had decided to go to the police and make his statement.

Richard Saunders, who lived in an old van on Edgwarebury Lane, also made a statement in which he described having seen both the accused in The *Boot* public house in Edgware on the night of the murder. According to Saunders he had asked them why they were looking 'so savage', to which 'Tiggy' had replied, 'There will be something up if anyone comes "mooshing" around our place.' Saunders was worried the tramps were referring to him, but was assured that they were talking about 'the Pigsticker'. Later that night he had heard a man repeatedly crying 'Oh! Oh!'

Fred Cozens, who lived in a shed on Edgwarebury Lane, knew the prisoners. He told the police he had been sitting on a bus with Ayres at Edgware Station that night, when Tiggy and Moosh had looked inside. Tiggy undid his coat and Cozens saw what he thought was an axe in his belt. Tiggy had nodded in the direction of Ayres and then the two men went away.

The accused appeared again the following Wednesday before a special sitting of the Hendon magistrates. J S Hogg presided and Charles Wallace presented the prosecution's case. J A Morley defended Shelley; and J M Lickfold appeared for Newman. The police presented evidence and once more the two tramps were remanded in custody. A week later they again stood in the dock and, this time, were committed for trial at the Old Bailey.

The case came to trial on Wednesday 24 June, before Mr Justice Swift. The outcome was a foregone conclusion as both defendants had effectively incriminated themselves through their statements. Even so, it is difficult not to feel a measure of sympathy for the two ageing rogues: both attempted to convince the jury the murder was justified because 'Pigsticker' had repeatedly stolen provisions from their shacks. One feels, upon reading the court transcripts, that they possessed only a rudimentary understanding of their predicament, and of the machinations of the law.

The following afternoon Shelley and Newman were found guilty of murder. On their being sentenced to hang Shelley remarked to the judge 'Thank you, Sir. It ought to have been done twenty years ago.' The condemned pair was led chuckling to the cells.

An appeal against the sentences was lodged but subsequently refused: Tiggy and Moosh were hanged in a dual execution at Pentonville prison on 5 August 1931.

A large part of Clay Lane remains today, looking much as it must have done in 1931. The author has tried to determine where exactly the tramps' colony was located, but has so far failed to do so. Clay Lane is a remote place, and can be a little scary if visited at night. Nevertheless, I would recommend a visit to the site: lines of large old sessile oaks march across the nearby grassland towards the motorway and the railway as they surge through the South Hertfordshire tertiary escarpment. If the reader *should* choose to visit, think of the two desperate men who once drank and stormed their lives away, high above the lights of the encroaching suburbs.

CHAPTER 16

The Stabbing of a Chocolate Girl

1936

I can't live without you. I would rather be dead.

The cinema came to Edgware in 1932, when the Ritz opened in Station Road. With its grand 'Egyptian' entrance and painted woodland settings in the interior, the Ritz promised to 'establish Edgware as the pivotal centre of a large and increasing district' and it proved to be a popular success. This was, after all, the golden era of the talkie. Yet the following account shows that this so-called 'Best of suburban picture houses' hid murderous rage born of jealousy or betrayal deep in its darkness.

The Ritz, Edgware, 1930s. LBB

Barbara Jesse Mant was an attractive and popular fair-haired nineteen-year-old. She lived with her parents in a small house in Edrick Walk, Burnt Oak and, until recently, had worked at Kemp's biscuit factory in West Hendon. In the spring of 1936 she took a job as a 'chocolate girl' at the Ritz cinema, where her mother also worked, serving customers in the tea lounge and selling sweets and cigarettes from a tray during breaks in the shows. Working at the cinema brought her more than just a wage however: she started dating the Ritz's commissionaire, James Hickling, thirty, who had been working there since March of the previous year.

Hickling, described as a tall, slight man with wavy fair hair, was required to stand in the street outside the cinema's entrance, wearing a uniform in order to impart a further element of grandeur to the ornate establishment. He was besotted with Barbara Mant the first time he saw her and had resolved to ask her out. In this he proved successful, the first date being an evening out at another cinema, the Regent in Burnt Oak. Hickling later said that he was very fond of the girl because, 'She reminded me of someone whose name I do not wish to mention, but who died.' The relationship rapidly developed into an intimate one, the couple consummating their relationship at Hickling's digs a month after they met.

Hickling lived close to the cinema, in Farm Road, Edgware, and should therefore have had no excuse for turning up late for work. However, he had a great thirst for alcohol and, in the summer of 1936, this was beginning to seriously affect his employment. A few days before the events described in this chapter Hickling was sent home from work for arriving late and for being drunk and incapable, and it is against this background that a murder – which deeply shocked the community – took place.

At that time there was a small recreation ground located between Deansbrook Road and Station Road, the exit being across Station Road from the Ritz. Today, there is a large branch of Sainsbury's on the site. Barbara Mant was in the habit of walking through the park in order to get to and from work, and up to a few weeks before her death Hickling would often accompany her. Unfortunately, in recent days their relationship had been in difficulties.

Perhaps Hickling was what we would nowadays describe as Barbara Mant's 'bit of rough'. Born in Swadlincote, Leicester in 1905, he left school at thirteen, working as a slagman at various mines and then as a labourer at a gas works and in a quarry. In 1925 he'd joined the army, serving in the 2nd Battalion the Queen's Guards. Despite being assessed as a 'clean and intelligent man' he managed to get himself discharged for being repeatedly absent without leave.

Barbara Mant's mother didn't approve of her daughter seeing the older man and this, together with Hickling's own alcohol-fuelled paranoia made him desperately insecure in the relationship. Worse, Barbara was now indicating that Hickling had a rival, a man known as 'Mick', though his real name was Arthur Henry Barfoot, aged twenty, who lived in Chandos Crescent, also in Edgware. Barfoot had actually been courting Barbara for some time prior to the events described here, but had been eclipsed in her eyes by Hickling. Recently, though, Barfoot's star had been in the ascendancy once more: he'd presented her with a ring, and had usurped Hickling's role as chaperone on Barbara's nightly journey home. Somehow the two men managed to keep the peace between themselves, even conversing when Arthur Barfoot arrived at the Ritz each night to pick up his girlfriend.

Despite surface appearances, feelings of frustration and rejection were building in Hickling – possibly this was behind his being sent home from the cinema. He began to bombard Barbara with letters and had taken to spending his time in the *Edgware Forum*, a drinking club on Station Road, where he sought solace in beer and whisky.

By all accounts, Saturday, 27 June 1936 was a hot day. Edgware would have been bustling with shoppers and, towards noon, the local pubs such as the *Railway Hotel* were filling with drinkers. *The Ritz* was showing a double feature: Katharine Hepburn and Cary Grant, in *Sylvia Scarlet;* and Jack Oakie in *Charm School.* It was also a day on which, according to Hickling's landlady, he seemed particularly upset about Barbara. Perhaps he had good reason to be: over the

Station Road, Edgware, 1930s. LBB

previous two evenings he had made an effort to force the issue with her, asking his landlady to speak to her on his behalf. But Barbara had reacted by returning his ring and choosing the much younger Barfoot as her fiancé.

Rejected by both girlfriend and employer, Hickling spent the early part of the afternoon drinking heavily in the Edgware Forum Club and in the *Railway Hotel* with Frank Young, a friend from The Ritz. It is worth pausing to consider Hickling's consumption of alcohol that afternoon, as later reported by various witnesses: at the Forum he consumed six glasses of ale, following this with a further five, plus two whiskies. Moving on to the *Railway Hotel*, he had three whiskies and, that evening he topped up with further booze in the company of his landlady. This was not a vast amount maybe, but it was sufficient to lower the threshold beyond which any ability to tolerate frustration becomes impaired. Certainly, Hickling was effusive concerning his woes. The manager of the Forum, Adolf Margulies, later recalled that Hickling showed him some love letters while at the club. Hickling told another friend, Frederick Pymm, that he had 'turned my job in over a girl.' Later that afternoon the two men visited a pawnshop where Hickling handed over a lady's engagement ring. Afterwards they went to the Edgware Hardware Stores where Hicklng purchased a large kitchen knife.

At one point Hickling approached Harold Hall, the cinema staff foreman at the Ritz and asked him to make representations on his behalf to Mr Harrison, the manager, about getting his job back. 'You will be able to start again tomorrow night, if you come in sober,' was the reply received.

Reports conflict over what happened that evening. It is known that Hickling returned to Farm Road to sleep off the alcohol, and that he was out again in the early evening drinking once more. According to Barfoot, Hickling was standing outside the Ritz at about 5.00 pm when he (Barfoot) picked Barbara up to walk her home for tea. At this point, Barbara momentarily left Barfoot to speak to Hickling, and he heard Barbara tell him, 'Don't let us cause a row here.'

Barbara was due for another spell on duty that evening, so Barfoot arranged to pick her up after work. This he did, arriving just before 10.00 pm and leaving with her a few moments later. Once again, Hickling was waiting, and this time he joined the couple as they crossed Station Road and entered the recreation ground. At some point Barbara turned round and asked Barfoot to leave her alone with Hickling, so while his companions had a heart-to-heart, he walked off to gaze over the fence at the railway. After about fifteen minutes he walked across to where Barbara and Hickling had been talking and was shocked to see his girlfriend on her knees, leaning against Hickling, who was lying across a fence. As Barfoot drew closer, they both stood up, and suddenly Barbara cried, 'He has got a knife!' At this, she grabbed at something with both hands and Barfoot saw something shining. Hickling then said, 'Go with Mick and I will use this on myself!'

Hickling then gave the girl two or three stabbing blows and she fell to the ground screaming and with blood pouring from her. Barfoot turned and fled the scene, hoping to find some assistance; Hickling immediately gave chase shouting, 'I'll do you next.' Barfoot ran out of the recreation ground and across to the Ritz, but seeing that his pursuer had disappeared, he quickly made his way to Edgware police station.

Shortly afterwards Hickling, blood-spattered and still holding the murder weapon in his hand, also arrived at the police station where he handed himself in. 'I come to give myself up,' he told the station's desk sergeant, 'for murdering a girl in the recreation ground opposite the Ritz cinema.' He was taken into custody as several officers departed, heading the two hundred or so yards to the recreation ground.

News of the tragedy quickly spread and a large crowd gathered. Three police vans and an ambulance arrived. Barbara was found lying face downward beneath some old oak trees in the north east corner of the ground. Her hands were crossed around her throat and her head was in a pool of blood. A paper bag containing fruit and a handbag were lying close by. First aid equipment was rushed to the girl, but it was too late.

The murder site was lit through the night as the police searched for evidence and, in the morning, Barbara's body was removed to the Hendon mortuary. Meanwhile Mr and Mrs Mant had arrived at Edgware Police Station to make statements, Mrs Mant collapsing with grief.

Hickling had already been searched and relieved of the leather knife sheath that had contained the murder weapon. He then made a full statement, in which he confessed to the killing:

Something snapped inside of me and everything went red. I remember striking her and saying goodbye. I knelt down intending to give myself the same, but I found there was no blade on the knife. I kissed her and ran away.

Hickling had indeed struck Barbara with such violence that the blade of the newly purchased knife had snapped off, and remained embedded in his victim's throat.

Early on Sunday morning, Hickling was charged with the murder of Barbara Jesse Mant. When asked if he had anything to say, Hickling replied, 'I wish I had done myself as well.'

On Monday, Hickling appeared at Hendon Magistrates' Court where he was charged with feloniously killing Barbara Jesse Mant. Only formal evidence was given and the prisoner was remanded until 9 July.

The following day the inquest was held at Hendon Town Hall before Dr George Cohen. A visibly shaken Mr Mant identified his daughter as the deceased, and then the result of the post-mortem was presented. The pathologist, Dr Temple Grey, told the inquest that death was due to haemorrhage from puncture wounds to the throat and back. 'Death was not very rapid and may have taken as long as twenty minutes,' he added. Divisional Detective Inspector Spash gave evidence regarding the arrest of Hickling and his being charged with murder. Dr Cohen then declared that the inquest was adjourned and that it was not his intention to resume it. With this, the jury stepped down.

The funeral of the victim took place on Monday, large crowds gathering at Edrick Walk as the funeral cortege departed. Barbara Mant was buried at Hendon Park Cemetery.

In the meantime, the police were busy taking statements from the friends and families of both the victim and the accused. When Hickling next appeared before the Hendon

The entrance to Hendon Park Cemetery, 2007. The author

Justices he was remanded to stand trial at the Central Criminal Court.

The trial at the Old Bailey began at 10.30 on 24 July, before Mr Justice Humphreys. L A Byrne appeared for the Crown, and Mr Thomas Carthew for the defence. In answer to the charge Hickling pleaded not guilty.

The first witness was Mr Mant who gave evidence of identification of the deceased. Barfoot was the prosecution's principle witness and repeated the evidence he gave at the police court.

The defence made some play over Barfoot's inability to recollect exactly what happened. The following is quoted directly from an account given in the *Hendon and Finchley Times:*

> *'Is it right to say your memory is rather vague as to what happened when the blows were struck'? – 'Yes.'*
>
> *'Are you able to say, on oath, with no uncertainty, that in fact Miss Mant did step back two or three paces when the blows were struck? You could not say that with certainty? – 'No, not with certainty.'*
>
> *'Did you know that Hickling had threatened to do himself in if he was unsuccessful in his suit for the girl?' – 'No I did not.'*

Frederick Pimm recounted going with Hickling to buy the knife, and Hickling's landlady stressed that the couple had been very fond of each other and that the accused had been very upset on the day in question.

Much was made of the love letters between the couple – more than two hundred were found in each of their respective homes – several being read to the court by the defence, presumably to secure a result of manslaughter or a plea to the judge for mercy from the jury. In one of these, sent shortly before Barbara Mant's death, Hickling had written:

> *My own darling sweetheart. I did not and can't realise that you have finished with me after seeing you go off with Mickey. I am at present half out of my mind. I love you, my darling, very much. I would give my life for you. I promise you that if it is I*

you have chosen, I will never let you down. I can't live without you. I would rather be dead.

Because Hickling's statements were highly incriminating the issue in court became one of intention and whether the defendant was of sound mind. Consequently, the proceedings were dealt with in little more than a morning. The jury retired in the early afternoon and quickly returned: Hickling was found guilty of murder.

'...And may the Lord have mercy on your soul –' Thus ended the trial of James Hickling. While the death sentence was being announced, Jesse Mant's father and Arthur Barfoot found themselves a quiet room in the court complex, preferring to sit in solitude rather than hear the solemn words.

In the event, however, Hickling proved to be lucky. The Home Secretary requested antecedents from the Commissioner of the Metropolitan Police and on 1 August approved a respite of capital punishment. James Hickling thenceforth began a life sentence.

CHAPTER 17

An Unhappy Suburb

1938–39

I don't know what made me do it

The years immediately following the execution of Tiggy and Moosh saw the lower, south end, of old Clay Lane widened and tarred over as part of the suburban development that became known as the Broadfields Estate, after a local farm. In fact, this part of Clay Lane was renamed Broadfields Avenue. Large numbers of houses now magically appeared where previously there had been fields and hedges.

The resulting influx of population inevitably brought tragedy in its wake, as will always occur where large numbers of people are grouped together. It is with two of these that we are now concerned.

Among the roads running off to the west from Broadfields Avenue are a series of concentrically arranged semi-circular streets. The outermost of these is named Franklyn Gardens and it was here, in April 1938, that the killing of Mrs Jesse Mitchell occurred.

Recently widowed, seventy-five-year-old Mrs Mitchell had moved into the semi-detached house about twelve months earlier. With her lived her unmarried daughter, Jean, forty-six, a Post Office supervisor based at Golders Green.

On Thursday 28 April a fourteen-year-old niece of Miss Mitchell had visited the house. Something really struck the girl as being seriously awry – though of what it was there seems to be no record – because when the niece returned to her home in Fulham, her mother felt moved to alert Edgware Police Station to possible events. In response, a police officer visited the house

Broadfields Avenue, Edgware, 1930s. LBB

to check if things were all right, but, unable to get a response to his knocks upon the door, he forced entry. Inside he found Jesse Mitchell lying dead in her bed; it was later determined that she had been strangled. Her daughter was found slumped in another room, unconscious from inhalation of coal gas.

The officer had a telephone message sent to Edgware Police Station and within a few minutes Inspector Baker arrived, accompanied by Inspector F Narborough, PC J Driscoll, and the divisional surgeon, Dr J E Ashby.

While the police were still in the house, another daughter of Mrs Mitchell arrived, together with her husband and child. Whether they were able to provide comfort to the slowly recovering Jean Mitchell, or needed succour themselves, we cannot tell. As is the way with many suburbs, the windows of the house had net curtains, and so few of the neighbours can have even been aware of the dramatic circumstances that had taken place within.

Jean Mitchell was presently driven to Edgware Police Station where she was interviewed by Inspector Narborough as to the circumstances leading to her mother's death.

After a night in the cells, in the presence of Superintendent Calver and Divisional Detective Inspector Spash, she was charged with the murder of her mother and with feloniously attempting to commit suicide by inhaling coal gas. Later that morning Jean Mitchell was driven to Hendon Police Court.

Here she appeared before the bench, the presiding magistrate being B E Higgis. Inspector Narborough was sole witness and Jean Mitchell was remanded for a week.

At her next court appearance, on 5 May, the magistrate described the case as a 'very tragic one, the facts of which are unfortunately all too plain.' Jean Mitchell was committed to the Central Criminal Court for trial.

The trial took place on 18 May in the famous Court One of the Old Bailey, before Mr Justice Humphreys. A large number of people from the Edgware area attended the court in order to see the trial but in fact the case was to be disposed of fairly quickly.

Three women served on the jury, and the prisoner was accompanied in the dock by a female prison warder as well as the customary two police officers. Jean Mitchell wore a dark suit and hat.

Mr L A Byrne, counsel for the prosecution, told the court that there were medical reports, and Dr J A Mackeson, Governor and Medical Officer of Holloway Prison was then called upon to give evidence. He stated that he had placed the prisoner under close observation at the hospital located inside the prison and had interviewed her frequently. Jean Mitchell was described as suffering from severe paranoid delusions. Mackeson added that the accused was obsessed with financial troubles, and that these worries had no basis in reality. He concluded that she was at present insane, unable to follow the course of the proceedings, unable to challenge a juror or to understand the evidence, or even to instruct counsel.

No further evidence was presented.

Mr Justice Humphreys addressed the jury on this issue, explaining that it was a principle of British law that no person could be tried for a crime unless that person was in a position to defend him or herself. Therefore a person who was so insane that he or she could not understand the proceedings could not exercise the right to challenge a juror, or follow the evidence. Neither could that person be expected to instruct counsel for defence. Such a person could therefore not be tried.

It was to be left to the jury to decide whether the prisoner was, or was not, fit to be tried by reason of insanity.

The judge added:

It is desirable that every prisoner should be tried, particularly when the prisoner is charged with murder. It is important to understand that, should the jury decide the prisoner is unfit to plea, this means that she has been neither acquitted nor convicted. Rather, the trial has been indefinitely postponed until the prisoner returns to a state of sufficient reason for the trial to proceed.

After a short consultation with his fellow jurors, the foreman stated that they found Miss Mitchell insane and that she could not plead. Justice Humphreys thereupon ordered that the prisoner should be detained 'until His Majesty's pleasure' and Miss Mitchell was lead from the dock.

The killing described below took place less than a year later in Central London, but the victim lived on the Broadfields Estate. What is particularly shocking is that the crime was committed against a complete stranger, and further, that the victim was a young schoolgirl.

Avril Ray Waters was a pleasant fourteen-year-old. Together with her parents and younger brother, she had lived on Broadfields Avenue for about two years. She was described as popular by all who knew her, and enjoyed a rich and varied social life. For instance, about a year before her untimely death, the Edgware branch of the League of Nations had staged a night of peace plays in which she had played the part of the Angel of Peace.

Waters had been attending Pitman's Shorthand College at Southampton Row, central London, and routinely travelled to and from college on the underground railway between Edgware and Tottenham Court Road.

On the evening of 15 February 1939, she was waiting on the northbound platform of the Northern Line at Tottenham Court Road for a train home, when she was approached by Leonard Ward Davies, aged thirty, a barman from Upper Holloway. Suddenly, and for no apparent reason, Davies pushed the unfortunate young woman under the wheels of an approaching tube train and then ran away up the platform.

Several passengers gave chase and Davies was quickly caught and pinioned. He was heard to repeat the phrase: 'I couldn't help it.'

The driver alighted and ran to where the girl was caught, still alive, underneath the second car of the train. Waters began to tell him her name and address before being taken to the Charing Cross Hospital where she died at 5.45 pm, the cause of death being multiple injuries.

The perpetrator was taken to the stationmaster's office where he told a police officer: 'I don't know what made me do it.'

Davies had evidently been feeling troubled for some time: a week before the killing he'd visited a work colleague and, clearly in a distressed state, asked him about his views on 'split personalities.' 'What would you think of a man who had an overwhelming impulse to throw somebody under a train?' he had added.

Avril Ray Waters was buried at the Jewish cemetery in Pound Lane, Willeseden on Friday, 17 February. A funeral cortege had picked up the coffin from Broadfields Avenue earlier that morning and set off down the Watford By-pass *en route* to the cemetery. Among the wreaths at the funeral was one from her college. The previous day Davies had appeared at Marylebone Street magistrates' court and been remanded in custody.

On 31 March Davies appeared for trial at the Old Bailey. The only witness to be called was Hugh Grierson, senior medical officer at Brixton prison, who'd had Davies under observation. He stated that in his opinion Davies was insane and unfit to plead or instruct counsel. The jury left the courtroom and then quickly returned, the whole trial taking less than ten minutes. Mr Justice Hawke ordered the prisoner to be kept in custody during His Majesty's pleasure.

As a result of two killings in such close proximity the Broadfields Estate must have been an unhappy suburb in the months leading up to World War Two. And neither does the story end there: as we will see, homicide returns to the area in 1949 when Daniel Raven batters his parents-in-law to death little more than a quarter of a mile from the homes of those involved in the cases we have just examined.

CHAPTER 18

He Wanted it All

1937

'Take me Guv'nor. I have done her in.'

Hardly had the Hickling case been laid to rest before Edgware once more played host to a killing. And, as in that case, 'love' was the fuel that fired the murderous impulse.

Walter Ernest Smee was a thirty-seven-year-old fishmonger, working in Whitchurch Lane, Little Stanmore. He had been born in Battersea in 1900, leaving school at fourteen to learn the fish trade. Clearly he was a brave man, joining the army at the age of fifteen to fight in France; when he enlisted he told the recruiting sergeant he was nineteen. The following year he was discharged after his mother reported the facts to the army. This probably saved Smee from an early death – but not from making a complete mess of the life thus saved. Photographs published in the *Hendon and Finchley Times* at the time of the events described in this chapter, show a tall, slightly stooping man with a receding hairline and yet, from all accounts, Walter Smee possessed a cheeky charm which women found irresistible.

Smee married in 1923 and three children followed in rapid succession. However, recent years had seen the marriage falter, and the couple had separated. While his wife remained in Rotherhithe with the children, Smee moved north in 1933, taking a house in Prescelly Place, a quiet suburban street just across Watling Street from Edgware-proper.

Despite the separation, Smee and his wife remained in contact. He had made tentative overtures concerning reconciliation, repeatedly inviting the family to come and join him at Prescelly Place. But all the while he had been seeing Alice Mary Hand, a married woman from Burnt Oak. Alice Hand had separated from her own spouse after the death of their son, who had been run over and killed by a lorry. She then became involved with Smee, and so far had their relationship progressed that she actually moved in with him at Prescelly Place on 15 November 1937. Before that she had been living in Watling Avenue.

The couple would seem to have been ill-matched; from all accounts Mrs Hand was something of a shrew. Walter Smee would seem to have been a man who wanted to please everybody, particularly himself, and Mrs Hand's temper must have received a more than usual amount of stimulation from Smee's announcement, shortly after she'd moved into Prescelly Place, that his wife and children were due to join them there. It was certainly asking a lot of both women to expect them to share a home with each other, and yet it is not entirely unprecedented. As we have seen, Goslett attempted to establish a similar suburban harem in Golders Green, in 1920, and with similar results. It is unclear whether Mrs Smee was aware of the exact nature of the pending arrangement, but the house in Prescelly Place must have seen some serious debate between the fishmonger and his common-law wife. Undeterred, Smee contacted a removals company based in Edgwarebury, and made arrangements for his wife, children and family furniture to be delivered on 24 November.

At about 5.45 pm on the fateful day the removals van pulled up outside Prescelly Place. Sitting alongside the driver, James Hughes, were Mrs Smee and her three children. In the back of the vehicle was the family furniture collected from Rotherhithe. The driver knocked at the door of the house but could get no reply. Suddenly he heard the screaming of a woman. Hurrying round to the rear of the house he peered through a gap in the curtains of a window. Inside he saw man standing, his hands round the throat of a woman lying across a chair. Suddenly the man let the woman go and she fell to the floor.

Alarmed, Hughes phoned the police and shortly constable D Smith arrived. Repeated knocking brought Smee to the front door. The constable insisted he gain entry to the house to see if everything was all right to which Smee replied: 'Take me guv'nor. I have done her in. She is in the front room. The ——— has caused a lot of trouble.'

Entering the house, the constable found the body of a woman lying on the floor in the front room. She was wrapped in a blanket. Another blanket was placed about her head and her hair was smeared with blood. Around the woman's neck was wound very tightly a length of wire from a wireless set. In the kitchen was found a coal hammer, also covered with blood.

Caught in somewhat embarrassing circumstances, Smee quietly agreed to accompany the constable to Edgware Police Station. As they departed a murder team arrived, together with the divisional surgeon, Dr J E Ashby.

The victim was, of course, Alice Hand. A post-mortem examination later revealed that she had died of a fractured skull. There were indications of eight distinct blows to her head, probably administered with the coal hammer. Dr Pitney, who carried out the examination, thought that the wire had been placed on her after death.

Following the gruesome discovery Mrs Smee and the children were taken to Edgware Police Station and then to Redhill Hospital, where they spent the night. Mrs Smee's shock at these unexpected events is easily imagined, but, mercifully the children remained unaware of the tragedy.

In the meantime Walter Smee had been subjected to the full attention of the Edgware police. Detective Inspector Spash makes another appearance here, taking initial charge of the murder inquiry. But shortly afterwards he was usurped by none other than Superintendent Yandell, one of Scotland Yard's 'Big Five' detectives, who in those days were making a reputation for themselves as arch-crime-fighters. Under questioning, Smee quickly admitted to killing Alice Hand and agreed to make a statement.

The resulting document makes for interesting reading. In it, Smee goes to considerable lengths to pitch himself as the unwilling recipient of Mrs Hand's demands. While fully admitting to having had a love affair with the woman, Smee claims that his ambition was always to return to his wife, but that Hand pushed him to finally divorce, and to marry her instead. After a period of separation, Mrs Hand had moved in with Smee, but it had been agreed upon that this was merely a case of friends sharing a house. Smee insists it had always been understood that Mrs Smee would eventually join them. Finally, on the evening in question they had a fierce row concerning the imminent arrival of Mrs Smee:

> *She threatened me and told me she would swing for me. She accused me of being the cause of her child's death…. I happened to say 'I'll go to the street door to see if I can see the van coming.' She said: 'Oh no you don't. She's not stepping her foot inside this house. I'm going to break your home up.'*

Smee then claims that a fight broke out between them. Hand attacked him with a hammer and, terrified, he fought back. He blacked out and could recall nothing else until he came to, kneeling beside her prostrate body.

Walter Ernest Smee was charged with the murder of Alice Hand and, after appearing at Hendon Police Court on 27 November, was remanded in custody. Two more appearances were made at the police court in the following weeks while the police built up their case. Smee's claim that he had acted in self-defence after rejecting Mrs Hand's unsolicited demands was seriously undermined after the police found some notepaper at Prescelly Place. On this was a 'letter to God' written in Smee's hand:

> *I have prayed often to You to let Alice Hand and myself be happy together in some place of our own. We love each other more than anything else on earth…. Alice Hand is the only one I love. Let her make me as happy as I hope to Make her in the near future – W. E. Smee.*

During the final appearance at the Hendon Police Court on 9 December, Smee was committed for trial at the Central Criminal Court.

The trial took place on 17 January the following year before Justice Goddard, the whole taking five hours. Mr G McClure and Mr Christmas Humphreys (son of the judge who had presided over the Rouse and Mitchell trials) conducted the prosecution. The defence was managed by St John Hutchinson KC. Smee appeared in the dock wearing a blue suit and white shirt and tie. He pleaded not guilty and retained his composure throughout.

In his opening speech Mr McClure described the home the accused ran in Edgware as a 'strange establishment' and proceeded to outline the events of 24 November. Evidence for the prosecution was then called. Alice Hand's husband testified that his wife had possessed a quick temper and had assaulted him a number of times. On one occasion she had hit the poor man on the head with a large iron.

Only one witness – Smee himself – was called for the defence. In a quiet, firm voice he outlined his life and then began to describe his relationship with Mrs Hand. 'My relations with her were intensely passionate, and I could not rid myself of the infatuation', he told the court.

> *'When I told her on the day of the tragedy that my wife was coming she flew into a violent temper, used bad language, and said she would swing for me. It seemed as if she was going to strike me with a hammer and she said, "I will kill you." I took the hammer away from her.'*

> Hutchinson: *'If you had not snatched away the hammer what would have happened?'*

> Smee: *'She would have been standing here instead of me. I snatched it away from her and hit her back. I remember hitting her twice on the head. I don't remember tying the wire around her neck. When I came to I was kneeling beside her with my arm about her.'*

In his concluding speech Hutchinson made a moving plea to the jury to reduce the charge of murder to one of manslaughter, arguing that Smee had already suffered the most appalling punishment anyone could have, in killing the one who meant everything in the world to him. Perhaps unsurprisingly the jury was unimpressed by this and after an absence of thirty-five minutes returned a verdict of guilty of murder, whereupon Mr Goddard donned his black cap and passed the sentence of death as required by law.

As Smee was led below, Mr Hutchinson asked the judge if it were possible for the prisoner to receive a visit from a clergyman and from his wife in the cells. Mr Goddard replied that while Smee could see the priest, a visit from his wife was conditional on prison regulations.

Yet Walter Ernest Smee did not suffer the hangman's rope. An appeal was lodged promptly and the case heard in February that year. The appeal contended that Justice Goddard, in summing up, failed to direct the jury as to the full weight of the provocation of Smee by Mrs Hand. The appeal was dismissed and with a shrug Smee turned and descended the stairs.

Shortly afterwards *The Times* reported that the sentence had been commuted to one of life imprisonment. On what grounds the Home Secretary requested the King's pardon I have been unable to ascertain.

CHAPTER 19

Shot at Point-blank Range

1941

*A bullet had gone through his cheek and at least
three more had penetrated his body.*

The years of the Second World War saw an unusually large number of murders committed in what later became the London Borough of Barnet: between 1939 and 1945 at least ten killings occurred within the area, though quite why this was so is difficult to determine. It is easy to assume that the wartime increase in mobility and the easy availability of firearms provided ideal conditions for killing. However, the years of the First World War – where these conditions also arose – were so quiet that the *Finchley and Hendon Times* felt moved to comment upon this when reporting the murder of John Thomas Gregory in 1919. Neither was the high murder rate confined solely to Barnet: nationally, 1942 marked an all-time high for murders and for crime generally. Possibly an element of social disintegration resulting from the Blitz was exacerbated by the fact the police were short of personnel. The blackout increased the difficulty of detection and created temptations which were difficult to resist, though this was not a factor in the case discussed here.

Late 1941 was a dark time for Britain and her allies. America had yet to enter the war, and in Russia a large German offensive had opened on 30 September and it seemed certain that Moscow would fall. As Soviet forces collapsed in the face of the German onslaught, the government in Moscow prepared to desert the threatened city. Nonetheless, Britain continued to hit back, and mid-October saw large bombing raids carried out against Nuremberg by the RAF.

On the Home Front severe food shortages intensified the mood of desperation and the *Hendon and Finchley Times* reported that local housewives were complaining about the difficulty of obtaining fresh fish. As part of the war effort, many residents of Hendon were 'digging for victory' by growing vegetables in allotments in order to assure a supply of some fresh food on their table: and it was a local man's generosity with the produce from his allotment that lead to the discovery of the following murder.

Moat Mount is a large hilly area of wooded land lying along the eastern edge of the A1, Barnet Way. Since the 1920s it had been designated as parkland by the then Hendon Council, and was popular with bird-watchers and courting couples. It is a gloomy sort of place, with footpaths climbing from the entrance through dense foliage towards Highwood Hill. A large lake is situated near the heart of the site and it was here, in a hut built specially for the park-keepers, that a ghastly killing occurred.

John (or 'Jack') Child had worked at Moat Mount since 1930. A semi-literate fifty-two-year-old, he guarded his province jealously. He had a reputation for making life difficult for any neophyte 'parkie' unfortunate enough to be assigned to

Moat Mount Lake, 1930. LBB

his 'patch', and on at least one occasion a work colleague had begged to be relocated away from him. Child had strong views on the preservation of the collection of exotic trees growing around the lake. These included Turkey Oaks and towering Wellingtonias planted by Edward William Cox, the owner of the estate of which Moat Mount was originally a part. Several times Child had come into conflict with his managers as a result of their attempts to thin out the numerous specimens. Child was also given to pilfering tools and lamps from bicycles parked at Moat Mount. He was known to steal packets of cigarette-papers from Notley's, a small tobacconist at Apex Corner, half-a-mile away. From all accounts he was also a bit of a peeping tom and enjoyed terrifying couples 'acting naughty' by sneaking up on them. But despite this lack of sophistication, Child had a mesmerising affect on women – particularly married women – and more or less openly consorted with them in his hut. He seems to have favoured the wives of well-to-do locals.

Friday 10 October was a wet and nasty day. At about 10.15 in the morning Horace Edward Druell set off from his home in Mount View, by Barnet Way, and wheeled his bicycle alongside that busy trunk road towards the entrance to the large park. He then headed up the path running from Barnet Way, past a line of hornbeams towards the lake. He was taking some vegetables grown in his allotment to his friend John Child. As Mr Druell approached Child's little hut, which was hidden behind shrubs close to the lake, he noticed that the door was open and, glancing in, started with horror. His friend was lying on the floor of the hut, his head and shoulders leaning against his chair; his face and clothes were splashed with blood and in his right hand he grasped a bloodstained dish cloth. Child's eyes were wide open, staring into the void – he was clearly dead. Turning about, Druell ran for help, making his way back down to Barnet Way where he pulled over a motorist, Mrs G Downing, who drove off to alert the police.

Detective Hawkins of S Division arrived about forty-five minutes later and was soon joined by other officers, including Detective Inspector Oxland of Golders Green and Detective Inspector Hare of Edgware. Examination of the body revealed that John Child had been shot a number of times at close range. A bullet had gone through his right cheek and at least three more had penetrated him elsewhere. He lay with his back propped up against a sideboard, suggesting that he had lived for a while after being shot, and the bloodstained dishcloth, with which he had presumably attempted to staunch the blood, supported this theory. Pieces from Child's dentures lay scattered about the floor of the hut where they had flown after the bullet had entered his mouth. The hut was searched for evidence and this quickly paid dividends. Five bullet holes had passed through the wall at the back of the hut and one lead bullet had remained embedded in the wood.

The police surgeon, Dr Robert Hunt Cooke, noted that Child had been dead more than twelve hours; this was verified when a search of the body revealed that the watch in Child's waistcoat pocket had been hit by a bullet and had stopped at 3.17. This helped the police to focus their inquiries on the previous afternoon in their search for witnesses.

The lead bullet mentioned previously was too damaged to be of use to the police. However, the bullet wedged in the watch was made of nickel and had survived its passage through Child's body fairly well. The round was identified as being a .455 calibre of a type fired from a Webley Revolver. The fact it was made of nickel was of great interest to the police, as nickel bullets had only been manufactured since the beginning of the current hostilities. Bullets of this type were reserved for use by the three services, and by Home Guard units. Many officers serving in Home Guard units had reactivated Webley service revolvers dating from the First World War.

Child's double-barrelled shotgun was found leaning against the wall of the hut. It was cocked but unloaded, and fresh fingerprints belonging to Child were found on its stock and barrel. A small cabinet containing ammunition for the gun was discovered to be partially open. This, to Hawkins, suggested that Child had attempted to defend himself during the attack.

Superintendent Cherrill and Inspector Birch of Scotland Yard dusted the hut for fingerprints, but only those belonging to Child and other members of the park staff, were found.

The body was removed to the mortuary at Hendon Town Hall, and a search of the grounds for the murder weapon and shell-casings was begun. The search involved a large number of people, including thirty police officers, a hundred local Home Guard members and a troop of boy scouts from the camp nearby. The lake was drained by the local fire brigade, the fish being removed to the Decoy Lake in Hendon. Police officers then climbed aboard punts and hauled these across the clay lake-bed as they raked the mud. At one point a luckless constable fell 'overboard' and sank up to his thighs in the ooze, having to be rescued by his colleagues using ropes. Despite all these efforts, nothing of any use was found.

The nickel bullet was sent for examination, and photographs were made of the marks scored on its side – every gun leaves a unique set of marks scored on a round fired from it – in order to provide a match should providence, or police prowess, ever provide the officers with a likely gun.

Sir Bernard Spilsbury carried out a post-mortem on the body that Saturday. Four bullets were found to have penetrated Child's body: one had entered his mouth, passing out through the right cheek, near the ear; another had entered his back near the spine, in the lumbar region, and had fractured one of Child's right-hand ribs before passing out through his chest – this was assumed to be the fatal shot; the bullet that broke the watch had initially entered Child's back, and had smashed his right kidney before exiting below the collar bone behind the waistcoat pocket. The final bullet had hit Child's right wrist before passing out of his body through the thumb. Spilsbury concluded that the wounds could not have been self-inflicted.

The following Tuesday the inquest opened for identification purposes. It was held by the Assistant Coroner, Dr A M Gorski, as Dr George Cohen was seriously ill in hospital, where he was shortly to die. William Herbert Child identified the body as that of his brother, and Detective Inspector Oxland told the jury that numerous inquires were still being made. Gorski then adjourned the inquest until 18 November.

In the meantime the police placed a request in the local press for anybody who had been in Moat Mount at the time to come forward. This enabled them to eliminate several potential suspects, but a couple seen that afternoon, around the time Child had been shot, were never found.

Child's life was scrutinised closely in a search for a motive. The picture that emerged was of a man who was paradoxically both sociable and private. Born in 1887, he had served in the army in the First World War, being invalided out in 1917. He had then travelled the country as a labourer and jack-of-all-trades. Child often drank at The *Rising Sun* public house at Highwood Hill, in Mill Hill, and also frequented the British Legion Club in Mill Hill Broadway where he drank with his landlord. He was very popular with the local children, often giving them sweets, and was generally described as cheerful. Several of his acquaintances expressed surprise at the murder, declaring that John Child hadn't had an enemy in the world. Yet a counter-image also emerged, of a man who was a compulsive womaniser, and who had a particular taste for the local married women. Chief Inspector Thorpe of Scotland Yard, who had since taken over the case, felt certain that it was Child's philandering that had provoked the murder.

John Child lived in digs at Birkbeck Road, in Mill Hill. His landlady, Emily Keene was viewed as having been a possible love-interest for Child, but, as the officer who interviewed her put it, 'she is a singularly unattractive woman, with bad teeth and hairs sprouting on her chin'. Her husband was a good friend of Child's and described the dead man as being 'like a brother to me'. The Keenes attended Child's funeral at Shooters Hill, and were clearly very fond of him.

An address book belonging to Child was found at Birkbeck Road and, from it, Chief Inspector Thorpe was able to draw up a list of six local women who were of interest to him; all of them were married, and all were suspected of having had illicit liaisons with the park-keeper at some point in the recent past. It should be added that the address book provided a mere fraction of the 600 plus people who were interviewed during the inquiry.

One of these, a woman living in Nan Clark's Lane, not far from the murder scene, was of particular interest. She was questioned closely but denied having had an affair with Child.

Her husband was also interviewed and admitted that he had held a grievance towards Child. He had been thrown out of the family home some months previously as a result of his drinking, and blamed Child's influence over his wife for his misfortune. However, he denied anything untoward having happened between his wife and Child. The interviewing officer didn't believe either of them, but both were able to provide alibis for the afternoon in question.

Another woman on the list admitted that there had once been something between her and Child, but that it had 'come to nothing' and had fizzled out some months before. She was able to give an alibi for her movements on 9 October and begged Thorpe not to inform her husband of her activities. Thorpe was happy to oblige. She went on to say that there had been some strife the previous year between Child and his landlord, Mr Keene, concerning an unpaid loan, and that, during 1940 Child had been very scared about something. On one occasion he had told her that he was worried something would happen to him. Keene was interviewed again and admitted that he had borrowed £5 off Child and had difficulty repaying it. He assured Thorpe that any differences had been cleared up subsequently and, although Thorpe was less then convinced, Keene had already given an alibi for his whereabouts on the day of the murder. He had been at work and had numerous witnesses to verify this.

Chief Inspector Thorpe systematically worked through his shortlist of suspects and found that all six women – and their husbands – were able to account for their whereabouts on the day in question. Casting about for a possible lead, the hapless Thorpe decided to look further back in time.

In 1921, Child had an affair with a woman named Emily Truman, whose marriage had broken up as a result. Could Child have been murdered by the enraged husband twenty years after the event? It was unlikely, but Thorpe couldn't afford to overlook the possibility. Mr Truman was interviewed but provided an alibi. Mrs Truman, who had since remarried, only learned of the case two years later but was also able to provide an alibi – she had been in hospital at the time, undergoing an operation for septic haemorrhoids!

Mr Truman had once travelled the country with Child in a van, doing labouring jobs. He recalled that their co-worker, Jimmy Lyons had disliked Child intensely, and had 'always been ready to cut Child's throat.' Lyons was found, but was also able to account for his whereabouts on the day in question.

Child's ex-wife Nora was shocked when informed of his death. They had married in 1909 and had two children. Nora Child had eventually fled her home, taking the children with her, as a result of Child's heavy drinking. She had not seen him for several years and had clearly played no part in his death.

Another suspect was Michael Ryan, who had been Child's manager for several months in the mid-thirties. Ryan had been assigned the job because he was something of a hard taskmaster and it was well known that Child was repeatedly late for work. Child deeply resented the younger man's drive to 'sort out' the dead and dying plants and trees in the park, and there were rumours the two men had come to blows in the boathouse by the lake. Child had complained to his brother William that Ryan was always trying to make him look small. He had accused Ryan of draining his duck pond out of spite. When questioned, Ryan denied this, claiming that although things had been difficult between him and Child, they had parted eventually on good terms. Only two weeks before the murder Ryan had asked Child to reset a scythe he had bought for gardening purposes.

The police weren't altogether satisfied and interviewed Ryan several more times. Further statements taken at the time reveal that Ryan had eventually been fired by Hendon Borough Council and that this had been based on a complaint made by a female visitor to the park. Ryan claimed in his statement that a former councillor had tipped him off that Child had set the whole thing up to get rid of him. Nevertheless, nothing more substantial than the possibility of motive could be levelled at Ryan and eventually the police had to pursue their inquiries elsewhere.

In an attempt to find the murder weapon the police scoured every Home Guard depot in an area extending from Wembley and Willesden to Watford and Bushey. Over two hundred and seventy service revolvers were collected and sent to the police laboratory at Hendon where test bullets were fired through them. The markings scored on these specially-designed soft bullets were compared with those found on the nickel bullet found in Child's waistcoat. However, no match was found.

A few days after the murder, a .455 Webley revolver had been discovered in a roadside ditch in Epsom. It was hoped that this would turn out to be the murder weapon. It was test-fired and, although there were striking similarities between this gun and the one with which Child had been shot, the match was felt to be insufficient to base any eventual prosecution upon.

When the inquest was resumed on 18 November, the police were no closer to making an arrest. Chief Inspector Thorpe informed the jury of how the police inquiry was progressing. The jury reached the only conclusion it reasonably could: without retiring to consider their verdict they decided that John Child was murdered 'by some person, or persons, unknown'.

With this, the murder was placed 'on the files' and was left open, as is usual in such cases. It was felt that the motive for the killing was probably revenge provoked by the deceased's improper associations with a married woman. No blame was attached to the police for doing their best under difficult circumstances. Several months later a summary of the case was sent to the Police Commissioner and this contained the following comment:

> *This has been an extremely difficult enquiry but despite the able and thorough manner in which it has been carried out by Chief Inspector Thorpe, no evidence is yet available to indicate the murderer.*

Nevertheless, the killer's escape from justice rankled the police, and echoes of the case persisted through the years following. Michael Ryan in particular remained a major suspect; so much so that, years later, in 1957, when an eleven-year-old boy in Edgware accidentally shot himself with his father's revolver the police took a more than usual interest. The boy's family name was Ryan. The boy had been injured by a .303 bullet fired from a .455 revolver. Could there be a connection between the boy's father and Michael Ryan? Had the murder weapon finally surfaced after all these years, presumably hidden away in a box in a cupboard, or tucked deep inside a chest of draws? In this, as in so much else in this case the police were to be disappointed. Despite having the same name, the two families were not related. Further, a study of the markings on the bullet failed to provide a match with those found on the bullet from Moat Mount.

CHAPTER 20

A Soldier Returns Home

1942

If I was your husband I would shoot you.

Despite the summer weather, Britain in mid-1942 was a gloomy place. The continued heavy losses to merchant shipping in the Atlantic exacerbated already severe food shortages. The bomb damage and endless queues for rations made life oppressive and difficult. On top of this the news from the front was not good. In the Soviet Union a major thrust by the Red Army had been resoundingly defeated at Kharkov, finally laying to rest the hope that the German Army was finished after the disaster before Moscow six months earlier. And in the Western Desert the Commonwealth forces were just about to lose Tobruk to Rommel's Afrika Korps after a stunning Axis offensive at Gazala. All in all, things could be described as a little difficult.

Reginald Irvine Chandler was definitely feeling moody about the state of the world: a combination of absent husbands and wartime shortages had driven many an English wife onto 'the game', and Chandler, twenty-three, had good reason to suspect his wife Victoria of being one of them. Since he'd volunteered for the army in June 1940, things had gone seriously wrong between them. Contact between the couple was intermittent due to the exigencies of war and the few periods of leave the young soldier had managed to take had been disastrous. Before the war, the couple had shared a home with Victoria's mother in Stanhope Road, Finchley. Since then, however, Victoria had moved out, leaving the two children with her mother, and had taken to sharing a flat in

Ballards Lane, North Finchley, 2008. Peter Simon

Ballards Lane with a Mrs Ling, a woman for whom Reginald Chandler had nothing but contempt. Even worse, when he had taken some leave back in 1941 with the intention of surprising his wife, Chandler had caught her and Mrs Ling with two soldiers in the North Finchley flat. As a result he had sent the children to a home in Scotland, and had taken to brooding on the situation.

Finally, in early June, Chandler decided he could take no more. After an interview at the barracks with his commanding officer, Major Carter, during which he'd managed to gain leave on compassionate grounds, Chandler 'borrowed' a .303 Lee-Enfield rifle from a corporal with whom he shared a hut. He had decided to teach his wife a lesson.

Chandler arrived in Finchley on the morning of 6 June, and made immediately for the small flat situated above an ironmonger's. Mrs Ling let him in and followed him upstairs to where Victoria was waiting in the kitchen. At first things seemed to be going well, the three sitting around the table drinking tea and making small talk. After a while Chandler asked Mrs Ling to leave his wife and him alone as they needed some privacy. Mrs Ling went downstairs and sat reading.

After about ten minutes she heard what she thought was a door slamming upstairs but, apart from glancing up momentarily, paid it no heed. A further ten minutes passed and then Chandler descended the stairs. Turning to Mrs Ling on the way out, Chandler said: 'If I were your husband I would shoot you.' Then he left.

Mrs Ling climbed the stairs to speak to her friend. Entering the kitchen she was greeted with the sight of Victoria Chandler lying face downward on the floor, blood streaming from her head. Mrs Ling ran from the flat to get assistance.

After leaving the flat Chandler had made his way to Finchley Police Station, about half a mile away. 'You had better go to Ballards Lane,' he told the desk sergeant while presenting him with the rifle, 'I have shot my wife.' As officers sped off to North Finchley to check Chandler's claim, he made a statement in which he described the events leading up to the shooting. He fully admitted to murdering Victoria Chandler and stressed that no-one other than himself had been involved. The police found a discharged cartridge case in the breach of the riffle and a further two undischarged rounds in Chandler's pockets; another discharged cartridge was later found on the floor at the flat. Detective Inspector Cripps took charge of the case and, looking over the scene in the kitchen at Ballards Lane, noted that a bullet which had passed through the kitchen window had left an indentation in the wall of a factory about fifteen yards away. This was duly noted in his report and, while researching this book, the present author was able to locate this bullet hole, still clearly visible after more than half a century.

Chandler was duly charged with murder and made an appearance at Highgate Court on 9 June before a bench presided over by Dr E A Ebblewhite. Chandler was remanded for a fortnight and granted legal aid. His next appearance on 24 June, during which he was defended by W Fordham, resulted in a committal to appear at the Old Bailey on the capital charge.

As we've said, life in wartime Britain was harsh and, perhaps out of concern to maintain perceived standards of moral

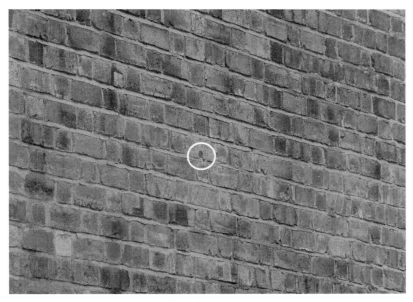

The bullet-hole in the factory wall, 2008. Peter Simon

behaviour in exceptional times, some sympathy was expressed for the soldier. When Chandler appeared at the Old Bailey in July, at the beginning of a two-day trial, even the prosecuting counsel Christmas Humphreys told the jury that the accused had 'possibly good reasons for jealousy'. Henceforward, everything seemed to favour the man in the dock. The victim's mother wrote to the judge expressing her regard for the man who had killed her daughter and urging the judge to order Chandler's release. This, of course, he could not do, and were Chandler to have been found guilty of murder, a death sentence would have followed. However, after hearing the evidence, the jury returned a verdict of not guilty of murder, but guilty of manslaughter. Chandler was sentenced to five years penal servitude, the judge scolding the undoubtedly relieved soldier: 'The Government provides rifles to engage the enemy, not to harm or frighten wives.' And with that, Chandler was lead below.

CHAPTER 21

The Body in the Marshes

1949

I killed Setty...and got away with murder.

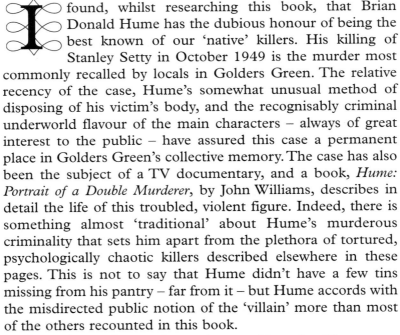found, whilst researching this book, that Brian Donald Hume has the dubious honour of being the best known of our 'native' killers. His killing of Stanley Setty in October 1949 is the murder most commonly recalled by locals in Golders Green. The relative recency of the case, Hume's somewhat unusual method of disposing of his victim's body, and the recognisably criminal underworld flavour of the main characters – always of great interest to the public – have assured this case a permanent place in Golders Green's collective memory. The case has also been the subject of a TV documentary, and a book, *Hume: Portrait of a Double Murderer*, by John Williams, describes in detail the life of this troubled, violent figure. Indeed, there is something almost 'traditional' about Hume's murderous criminality that sets him apart from the plethora of tortured, psychologically chaotic killers described elsewhere in these pages. This is not to say that Hume didn't have a few tins missing from his pantry – far from it – but Hume accords with the misdirected public notion of the 'villain' more than most of the others recounted in this book.

There is an interesting twist to this tale: Hume was originally found not guilty of murder but later admitted to the crime, protected as he was by the then law of double-jeopardy whereby he could not be prosecuted twice for the same offence.

On Friday, 21 October 1949 Sydney Tiffin, a farm labourer, went punting on the marshes at Tillingham, Essex. Tiffin was looking to shoot some wild fowl but was interrupted in his hunt when he saw a grey object floating in the water. He later described this as looking like a bundle of bedding tied with string. Upon cutting the string he was horrified to see part of a human body float out.

Tiffin fastened the corpse to a stake and made haste to the police station at Bradwell-on-Sea. Within hours the Essex Constabulary had retrieved the headless, legless corpse and it was taken to the mortuary at St John's hospital in Chelmsford where a Home Office pathologist, Dr Francis Camps, performed the post-mortem.

The body was of a middle-aged male who had been in reasonable health up to the time of his death. Death was due to stab wounds in the chest. After death the ribs had been fractured by a 'crush-type' of injury and the legs and head severed with a sharp instrument, and the bones sawn. It was obviously important that the police identify the body, not least in order to find his killer. Skin was removed from the corpse's hands and taken in a jar to New Scotland Yard by the officer assigned to the case, Detective Inspector Totterhall. Prints were taken from the skin and by comparing these with samples filed in the criminal records the victim was identified as Stanley Setty, a second-hand car dealer from Warren Street. Because the victim came from London, Detective Inspector Totterhall requested that the Metropolitan Police become involved in the case. They did, and Detective Sergeant Sutherland and Superintendent MacDougall were assigned to the inquiry.

Setty had been reported missing on 5 October by his brother-in-law. For some reason the police seem to have shown a real concern for Setty's well-being. It was known that he had travelled out to Watford for business reasons on 4 October and that he had received £1,005 in £5 notes after cashing a cheque. Two hundred of the notes were numbered in series, M41039801 to M41040000, and a notice had been issued through the press requesting members of the public to look out for these.

Stanley Setty was born in Baghdad in 1903. He had been prosecuted for currency offences a few years previously and had also been linked with gunrunning to Palestine during the Israeli War of Independence. Perhaps it was precisely this underworld background which had caused the police to be so worried for him. A man like Setty would have dangerous enemies. The identification of the body found at Tillingham confirmed the police in their anxieties.

On 24 October a breakthrough occurred in the murder inquiry when John Herbert Simpson, a director and chief engineer of United Services Flying Club at Elstree aerodrome, contacted the police insisting he could help. According to Simpson, on 5 October a man, Brian Donald Hume, had visited Elstree, arriving in a black Singer motorcar, and paid an overdue account of £20 in five-pound notes. He also hired a plane, an Auster, registration number G-A. GXT, and had taken off, saying he was flying to Southend.

The following day, 6 October, Hume arrived back at the aerodrome by chauffeur-driven car. He stated that he'd left the hired plane at Southend aerodrome and that he was going to collect it and fly back to Elstree later. He picked up his Singer and set off. Later that day a message was received from Air Control at Gravesend aerodrome notifying Simpson that the plane had made an unscheduled landing there owing to weather conditions. When Simpson inspected the plane a few days later he noted that the port window was damaged, its front sliding portion being jammed so as to render it impossible to close.

Chief Inspector MacDougall followed up this line of inquiry. Upon questioning other staff at Elstree aerodrome, two of them recalled seeing Hume load two bulky parcels into his plane before taking off. These were described as being wrapped in brown-coloured material wrapped in string.

The next day MacDougall travelled out to Southend and, accompanied by Detective Inspector Totterhall, questioned staff at the aerodrome. A taxi driver recalled having driven Hume back to his home in Golders Green and he had noted the thick bundle of five-pound notes carried by the man. By luck a fitter from Elstree happened to have been at Southend at that time. Hume had recognised him and asked him to fly the Auster back to Elstree for him. The man refused. He noted that there were no parcels aboard at that time.

The two officers then took a short round trip in an Auster to see if it were possible to throw a parcel out without air-resistance interfering with the process. This, they found, could be done without undue difficulty.

The Criminal Record Office contained files showing that Hume, born in Burnham-on-Sea, Somerset, twenty-nine years before, had 'form' for petty theft, dating back to before World War Two and that, during the war, he had been prosecuted for impersonating an RAF officer and for committing various black-market offences. He was also the registered holder of a flying licence, issued in 1948.

A case was building up against Hume and it was decided to interrogate him. On 26 October Chief Inspector John Jamieson, accompanied by Detective Inspector Davies of D Division, visited Hume at his second, and third-floor flat in Finchley Road, close to the Ionic Cinema (now Sainsburys), in Golders Green. Officers were posted behind the block of flats in case the suspect tried to escape, and Jameson and Davies knocked on the front door.

Finchley Road, Golders Green, 2008. The author

'What is this all about?' Hume asked upon being confronted by the two police officers. Jamieson told him that he was not prepared to discuss the case while standing on Finchley Road and suggested they go to the police station. With this Hume was taken to Albany Street Police Station where MacDougall asked him to account for his movements around the time of Setty's disappearance. Hume replied, 'This is going to be difficult.'

Hume initially claimed he had no clear recall of the time in question and that he had never heard of Stanley Setty. He admitted he had driven to Elstree, and that he had hired the Auster, but denied knowledge of any parcels. At this stage he was confronted with the testimony of the witnesses from Elstree and Southend. Hume placed his head in his hands and said: 'I'm several kinds of a bastard, aren't I?'

In an attempt at damage limitation Hume then made a lengthy statement in which he claimed a man named Green – also known as 'G' – had approached him in Warren Street on 4 October. According to Hume, 'G' along with an accomplice named 'Mac' asked him to do a job for them, a job requiring Hume's piloting skills. They wanted him to fly out over the Channel and ditch some steel plates that had been used in the printing of counterfeit ration coupons. Hume agreed to do this for them and 'G' and 'Mac' forwarded cash in advance for the job; £100 in £5 notes.

The next day, 5 October, Hume hired a car from Saunders garage in St Alban's Lane, just around the corner from his flat. At about 10.00 am the two men turned up at his flat accompanied by a third character named 'Boy'. They brought two bulky parcels with them and Hume claimed he stored these in a cupboard, away from the prying eyes of his wife. He asked his visitors why they didn't just bury the plates and offered to do it for them but they insisted they wanted the items buried at sea. Hume was told that a third parcel would also need to be disposed of and would be delivered the following day.

Later Hume drove the two parcels out to Elstree aerodrome and flew them to a spot to the east of Southend Pier, ditching them into the Thames Estuary. He then landed at Southend and took a taxi back to Golders Green to pick up the third parcel, which was delivered by 'Mac'. He hired a chauffeur-driven car back to Elstree to collect his Singer and then returned to Golders Green, hiring a help from Saunders Garage to load the bulky item into the car. He had then driven to Southend, loaded the parcel into the Auster and disposed of it in the same manner as the first two packages. Unfortunately he had underestimated his fuel-consumption, and on the way back to Elstree he had been forced to make an emergency landing at Gravesend.

He claimed he'd read of Setty's disappearance in the newspapers, and that it had crossed his mind that the parcels could contain his body. Hume also admitted that he'd met him once, about six years previously, when Setty had sold him a car.

In order to check Hume's statement the police scoured the area around Warren Street looking for the three men described but it came to nothing. According to MacDougall, in his report to the Chief Superintendent, written shortly after the case had been to court, this was because 'it is almost certain that no such men ever existed'.

On 28 October Hume was charged with having murdered Stanley Setty some time between the fourth and the sixth of the month. Hume was adamant he was not the murderer, answering to the charge with the words, 'No, I didn't kill him. I am not guilty.' He was promptly remanded in custody from Bow Street Magistrates' Court. A subsequent appearance resulted in a committal for trial by jury.

Meanwhile the police enquiries continued, establishing that contrary to Hume's claims, he'd had an ongoing association with Setty. Two of Setty's business friends testified to seeing the two men talking together at Setty's garage in Cambridge Terrace Mews, W1, as recently as mid-August.

An Essex boatman was interviewed concerning the possibility of a parcel dumped in the Thames to the east of Southend turning up at Tillingham. In his opinion this was possible.

Hume's wife, Cynthia made a statement in which she claimed no recollection of the men visiting her husband, or of him ever mentioning being placed under pressure by anybody.

The investigating officers also began to uncover a motive: a study of the prisoner's accounts revealed that he had been in financial difficulties for some time and that he had been borrowing money and taking out loans as well as reneging on payments due. All this had begun to change the day Setty had been reported missing. Hume had opened a savings account at Golders Green Post Office back in 1942. Towards the end of August 1949 he had requested that he be allowed an overdraft of £70 until 14 September, and this had been agreed to. On 27 September Hume's account was overdrawn to the extent of £78.0s.5d and on 5 October Hume paid £90 into the account. On the same day £50 was paid into Cynthia Hume's account at a bank in Edgware Road, this being paid in £5 notes. He paid off £9 owed to a Golders Green barber since September. He'd also owed the local branch of WH Smith £5.4s.3d for newspapers and paid off the bulk of this with a £5 note.

A business concern controlled by Hume, Little Atom Electrical Products of Hay-on-Wye, owed £667 to another company with which they'd had dealings and Hume had been pressed on this and threatened with proceedings.

Type 'O' blood had been found behind the pilot's seat in the aircraft used by Hume. This corresponded with Setty's blood type. Even more damning was forensic evidence uncovered during a search of Hume's flat. The same blood type was found on the floorboards at Finchley Road and also on the edges of the linoleum in the bathroom. A green carpet was stained with human blood but dyeing and cleaning rendered it impossible to determine of which type. However, the Humes' cleaner, Ethel Stride, recalled noting the carpet missing on 5 October. A local dry-cleaning company, Burstal Cleaners of Finchley Road, had received the carpet from Hume on that date along with a request for it to be cleaned and dyed. According to the Manageress, the issue of the carpet had caused considerable anxiety for Hume who had harassed her about it until its return on 19 October.

Finally, an employee at Saunders Garage had helped Hume stain some floorboards at the flat on or about 7 October.

Hume's trial began on 18 January 1950 at the Old Bailey. As with so much else in this story, events in the court refused to proceed in a straightforward manner. A jury was sworn in and the counsel for the prosecution, Christmas Humphreys, outlined the case. Several witnesses had already appeared when, on the second day, disaster struck. The judge, Mr Justice Lewis fell ill and had to be rushed to hospital, his place being taken by Mr Justice Sellars. The jury was discharged and sworn in again.

Throughout the trial Hume stuck to his story that he had not seen Setty on the day of his murder. He also maintained that the bloodstains had come about because of the parcels having been in his flat.

The defence managed to find a witness who admitted to having worked in Paris with a gang of car smugglers. His description of the men, and some of the names, seemed to accord with Hume's story. The jury retired at noon on 20 January. It took less than three hours for an astonishing verdict to be announced – they all failed to agree. This was in the days before majority verdicts were required for a guilty verdict and the jury's failure to reach a unanimous decision was disastrous for the prosecution. An immediate retrial was ordered, the Crown changing the indictment to one of 'being an accessory after the fact to murder'. Hume, clearly deciding to quit while ahead, pleaded 'guilty' to the charge.

Hume was sentenced to just twelve years in prison. His wife quickly filed for divorce and formed an unlikely liaison with pioneering *Evening Standard* crime journalist Thomas Webb. They eventually married in September 1958, shortly before Webb's death from Leukemia.

Hume was released on parole on 1 February 1958 and, in an early example of chequebook journalism, sold his story to the *Sunday Pictorial,* the 'Newspaper for the Young at Heart.' The six-week series on Hume began its run on 27 May that year. It makes for extraordinary – and occasionally hilarious – reading. 'I Killed Setty…And Got Away with Murder' reads the headline in the first issue:

I, Donald Hume, do hereby confess to the Sunday Pictorial that on the night of October 4, 1949, I murdered Stanley Setty in my flat in Finchley Road, London. I stabbed him to death with a dagger while we were fighting.

Hume goes on to tell his life story. According to him, his mother abandoned him shortly after birth and he was paced in an orphanage. Life there had been tough, the children being subjected to abuse; and punishments included being locked in a filthy, dank cellar for hours on end. Often eight children would sleep in an iron bed and food was sparse. As a result Hume developed a chip on his shoulder and decided to 'get back' at a world which had treated him so badly. Despite being married at the time of the murder, and being a new father, Hume admits that his real love was his pet Alsatian dog, Tony. He claims that the reason he killed Setty was because the second-hand car-dealer had made the mistake of striking the dog during a visit to Finchley Road to discuss business.

Hume had been spray painting and selling stolen cars on Setty's behalf for several months. Tony accidentally ruined a re-spray job on one of Setty's stolen cars which prompted Setty to kick the dog in a fit of rage. Hume brooded on this, and saw red a few days later, when Setty accused him of pocketing some money due to him. The two men came to blows in the Finchley Road flat, Setty quickly gaining the upper-hand. Fearing for his life, Hume grabbed an SS ceremonial dagger he had bought from a friend and kept as a 'souvenir' from the war years:

> *The handle of the dagger glinted in the light. I could see the initials 'S.S.' In war they stood for* Schutz Staffel, *the elite army corps of Nazi Germany. Now those S.S. initials stood for forty-four-year-old Stanley Setty.*

Hume claims he merely intended to scare Setty into letting go of him, but that he succumbed to his rage after being taunted by his opponent. He repeatedly plunged the knife into Setty until, soaked with the other man's blood, he was left with a corpse to dispose of. Calming down, Hume hit on the idea of throwing Setty's remains out of an aircraft.

He then describes how he cut Setty's body into portions, the better to dispose of the remains. I will spare the reader the gruesome details – suffice it to say, he had to purchase a hacksaw and lino-knife to carry out the task. He then hired the

Singer car and drove to Elstree with the first two parcels, noting that the approach to the aerodrome took him along *Dagger* Lane!

His dog, Tony, accompanied him on his mission to dispose of the third parcel. There is a photograph included in an issue of the *Sunday Pictorial,* of Hume leaning out of the Auster's window, a parcel falling away into the Thames, and a superimposed picture of the dog sitting in the aircraft's rear compartment.

Another interesting twist to the tale surfaced years later: Hume admitted that he'd based the descriptions of the three men he claimed had hired him to dispose of the parcels, on the three police officers who were questioning him at the time.

Hume received £2,000 from the *Sunday Pictorial* for his story: it did him no good. In no time he was wanted for committing a bank robbery in Brentford. He escaped to Zurich where he frittered away his money in nightclubs and restaurants. A further robbery, this time at the Gwerbe Bank in Zurich, resulted in the fatal shooting of a taxi driver. Hume was captured by the Swiss authorities and imprisoned for life. In 1976 he was transferred to Britain and placed in Broadmoor, the top-security hospital for the criminally insane.

CHAPTER 22

A Case of Post-war Sleaze

1949

I did not do it.

It took a while for a Jewish community to establish itself in Edgware. As late as 1930 there were reckoned to be only thirty Jewish households in the area, but this changed in the years either side of the Second World War with families moving to the suburb from the East End. The relatively spacious streets of Edgware must have seemed like paradise after the crowded warrens and alleyways of Whitechapel. Most of the Jewish population consisted of hard working and decent folk. However, as in any community, this was not invariably so: the following account is a case in point.

On the surface everything looked fine in Daniel Raven's life. Married to a woman from a wealthy family, and shortly to become a father, Raven lived in a large house on Edgwarebury Lane, to the north of Edgware. His parents-in-law, Leopold and Esther Goodman, lived close by, in Ashcombe Gardens on the other side of the Watford By-pass. Mr Goodman had not only given the hand of his twenty-two-year-old daughter Marie to Raven in marriage, but had also employed him briefly at his electrical goods firm, L Goodman Radio Ltd, situated in Percy Street, Soho. With a new grandchild and a thriving business, Russian born Goodman must have been very happy with the way things were going. Recently Raven had moved on from Mr Goodman's employ and had begun working as an advertising agent. So far, so ordinary, yet the events of October 1949 were once again to provide the public with a grisly reminder that horror lurks in the most unsuspected of places – in this case, the quiet middle-class streets of Edgware.

Daniel Raven was twenty-three, a good-looking man with auburn hair and a somewhat stylish dress sense. He grew up in Stoke Newington and, after the war, lived for a while in Hounslow. During the war Raven had served in the RAF, and after suffering injury in a plane crash – from which he was the sole survivor – he was given a discharge on medical grounds. His family had been moderately successful: at the time of the events described here, his father lived in Brim Hill in the Hampstead Garden Suburb, and now Raven had married into money.

On the evening of Sunday, 5 October 1949 Marie Raven gave birth to a baby girl at the Strathlene Nursing Home in Creighton Avenue, East Finchley. She was visited nightly by both her doting husband and her parents. On 10 October her husband visited her as usual, being joined later by Mr and Mrs Goodman. At about 9.00 pm the Goodmans departed in their car and were followed shortly after by their son-in-law.

Nobody will ever be sure what happened later that night, nor why. But what is certain is that Daniel Raven gained access to the Goodman home and went berserk, battering the couple to death with the heavy base of a television aerial. He then drove the short distance to his house and attempted to dispose of his blood-splattered suit by stuffing it in the boiler, to burn. Presumably he felt that he had a little time to straighten himself out and calm down sufficiently to feign shock when the bodies were eventually discovered. If so, then he was mistaken. At about 10.30 pm his doorbell rang. Raven must have been horrified to find that his unexpected visitors were Mrs Goodman's brother-in-law, Frederick Fraiman and his wife. Something awful had happened at Ashcombe Gardens, they told Raven, and insisted he accompany them back to the Goodmans' house. Raven was in no position to make excuses. Before leaving his home he put on a fresh suit, shirt and tie.

What had led to such a rapid discovery of the crime? Simply put, Raven had been unlucky. Purely by chance the Fraimans had called at the Goodmans' shortly after his departure, the purpose of their visit being to enquire how Raven's wife and

Ashcombe Gardens, Edgware, 2007. The author

baby were getting on. Unable to gain access, Mr Fraiman had climbed into the house through an open window, his wife following close behind. Inside they found the battered couple. Mrs Goodman was dead, and Mr Goodman suffering from very serious head injuries. The horrific find was too much for Mrs Fraiman who ran screaming along the street. Her cries of 'Murder! Murder!' brought neighbours running out of their houses.

At 10.02 pm Mr Fraiman phoned the police 'using the 999 system', as the *Hendon and Finchley Times* later described, and within two minutes PCs Hill and Hobbs arrived in an area patrol car. Detective Superintendent Peter Beveridge, head of Scotland Yard's Murder Squad, who lived close by, followed them shortly after. While the Fraimans dashed off to inform Raven of the unfortunate event, the police set up a murder inquiry.

Ashcombe Gardens is a quiet street leading off of Edgwarebury Lane, to the south of the Watford By-pass. Supposedly of quality, the dark brick houses somehow manage to be squat and ugly, although they exude an aura of vulgar wealth. By the time the Fraimans arrived back there together with Daniel Raven, the street was jammed with police vehicles and onlookers.

In the meantime, Mr Goodman had expired despite the best efforts of a local doctor to save him. Detective Inspector Diller had joined Detective Superintendent Beveridge and the two constables. A search of the house uncovered the bloodstained base of the television aerial in the pantry sink – the fact the Goodmans had a television set in 1949 indicates how wealthy the couple were. The initial assumption was that a burglar had attacked the Goodmans, and yet there was no sign of forcible entry anywhere in the house. A safe was located but had not been interfered with in any way; it was later found to contain a substantial amount of money.

When the police confronted Raven with the news of the Goodmans' deaths he put on a great show of emotion. 'Why did they tell me to go?' he cried. 'Why didn't they let me stop?' He sat on the stairs and burst into tears whereupon Diller told him to pull himself together. Raven then launched into a long monologue about how the Goodmans had been terrified of being burgled. Yet despite this, the young man claimed, they had begged him to leave them that evening. When asked to describe his relationship with the victims he stated that he didn't get on badly with Mr Goodman, 'but Mrs Goodman and me didn't get on too well'.

Perhaps Raven overacted in expressing his concern for the murder victims, or perhaps his performance lacked some element of vitality, thus revealing an undercurrent of loathing. Either way, suspicions began to grow in the minds of the officers present. Diller's suspicions increased when told that, according to witnesses at the nursing home Raven had been wearing a dark blue suit earlier that evening, not the grey one he wore at Ashcombe Gardens. Raven's shirt was also noticeably fresh and clean. Diller decided to question the young man further.

Raven was asked to accompany the officers to Edgware Police Station. Diller also requested that he hand over his house keys. The suspect did so, commenting: 'but you won't find anything there. I only had a bath'. At the station Raven made a statement under caution in which he repeated his initial claim, that he had left the Goodmans in good health at Ashcombe Gardens earlier that evening.

Diller entered the Raven home at about 11.00 pm the same evening, and quickly found the bloodstained suit still smouldering in the boiler. Later it was found to be spotted with blood from the Goodmans' rare blood group AB. A pair of bloody shoes found in the garage would reveal the same result. Early the next morning Diller returned with Commander Hugh Young, Assistant Police Commissioner, from Scotland Yard. Dr Donald Teare, a Home Office pathologist was also in attendance. Further traces of group AB blood were found, both in the house and in Raven's car.

Things were beginning to look bad for Daniel Raven. One can imagine his feelings on being confronted with this evidence. It was now necessary for him to change his story drastically and this he did, admitting in a further statement that he had been to Ashcombe Gardens after the murder was committed and had panicked upon finding the bodies of the Goodmans. He had knelt besides the couple, he said, and this was how the blood had got onto his clothes. When asked why he failed to contact the emergency services, Raven merely reiterated that he panicked.

At 6.30 on the morning of Tuesday, 11 November, Detective Chief Inspector Albert Tansill charged Daniel Raven with the murder of Mr and Mrs Goodman. Raven protested his innocence, answering 'I did not do it' in response to the charge. He claimed that his father-in-law had made enemies through crooked business deals. The following day the accused appeared at a special sitting of Wealdstone Magistrates' Court. All available seats were taken in the public gallery, and onlookers gathered outside, hoping to catch a glimpse of the accused. Raven, who stood throughout the hearing, wore a smart brown bird's-eye suit. Mr S Rutter represented him. The prisoner was charged that on 10 October he murdered Leopold Goodman, aged forty-nine, and Esther Goodman, aged forty-seven. Tansill gave evidence before the court. Raven was remanded in custody for eight days. He was granted permission to speak to his father.

While Raven was in custody the police worked hard to build up a case against him. Chief Superintendent Beveridge was placed in charge of the inquiry and co-ordinated police work. Establishing a motive for murder proved difficult. Robbery obviously featured as a possibility, yet no money had been removed from the Goodmans' safe. Despite Raven's display of emotion, had there been tensions between him and the Goodmans? This was to be the theory upon which the police based their inquiries. Establishing a motive was deemed to be important in this case because without this any eventual prosecution would have to rest on forensic evidence. Despite having the bloodstained suit the police experienced difficulties gathering further evidence. Fingerprinting could not provide sufficient evidence for a prosecution: because Raven was a regular visitor to the house, his prints were everywhere.

In their search for a motive the police looked into the respective backgrounds of both victim and suspect. This provided tantalising evidence of criminality on the parts of all concerned.

A Mr Samuel Vespor of Peckham had had dealings with L Goodman Radio Ltd some time previously. In a statement made to police officers he recalled that, at that time, Raven was acting as sales representative for his father-in-law. On one occasion Raven had admitted to Vespor that he stole stock from Goodman on a regular basis and tried to lure Vespor into a discreet sales arrangement of benefit to both of them.

Moved by his conscience, Vespor told Mr Goodman of Raven's comments when they next met. According to Vespor: 'Mr G broke down and said "a crook in the family. I can't believe it. What am I going to do?"'

Vespor then recalled Raven phoning him and saying: 'Do you know Mr Vespor, one of these days I'm going to get all that I want, even if I have to do the old man in to get it!' He then said: 'I have so little money and Mr Goodman has so much. Why should this be?'

A picture rapidly emerged of Raven as an unstable and potentially violent character. Fraiman described Raven as a man of moods with a terrible temper. The Ravens' neighbour told the police she had heard many late-night rows between the young couple, arguments that often ended in furious displays of anger towards his wife on the part of Daniel. Raven had also suffered a nervous breakdown about six months after his marriage to Marie.

Mr Goodman was no angel either. Inquiries showed that he had been involved in various breaches of currency regulations two years before his death. Suggestions arose that possibly he had crossed somebody during this time and had been assassinated as a result. While this was considered a possibility, there was no evidence of such an occurrence forthcoming, whereas there were substantial links between Goodman's murder and Daniel Raven.

Various complex civil cases followed on from the arrest of Raven: the Raven and Goodman families quarrelled over who should have access to the safe found in Ashcombe Gardens, which was now in the safekeeping of the police. A similar argument broke out concerning the contents of the house in Edgwarebury Lane. This merely intensified the police's impression that there was something hard and ruthless about the whole set-up.

Raven made three appearances at Hendon Magistrates' Court over the following few weeks, the police presenting more evidence at each hearing. Finally, after forensic evidence concerning the murder weapon and other matters was presented, he was committed for trial at the Central Criminal Court.

The trial of Daniel Raven began at the Old Bailey on Tuesday, 22 November before Mr Justice Cassells. Anthony Hawke KC appeared for the Crown with John Maude KC acting as Raven's defence. Raven was charged solely with the killing of Leopold Goodman. Over 200 people were crammed into every inch of seating and standing space throughout the trial; something in the grim events at Ashcombe Gardens had gripped the public imagination.

Due to the absence of any clear motive for murder, the prosecution focussed on the bloodstains found on Raven's suit and in his car. The fact the accused had changed his clothes between leaving the Goodmans and his return was also presented to the jury. Raven's motive for killing the Goodmans was deemed to be of less importance and, in fact, was never clearly defined. The defence made great play of Fraiman's inheriting the business from Mr Goodman, as if to place a possible motive for murder elsewhere other than at the hands of Raven.

Needless to say, the jury were not impressed; after a trial lasting three days they filed out to consider their verdict. The accused was sent down to the cells, and a little less than an hour later the jury returned. The atmosphere in the court was electric as Raven resumed his place in the dock. A deathly silence fell on the crammed courtroom, broken only by the sound of a woman sobbing high in the public gallery. The judge asked the jury for their verdict. He received the reply: 'guilty' and, donning the black cap, turned to face Raven. The prisoner gripped the edge of the dock as the death sentence was read out and, visibly shaken, was helped down into the cells by two police officers. Justice Cassells then thanked Detective Inspector Diller for his fine investigative work, the policeman countering that he was anxious not to take the full credit.

Shortly after the trial Marie Raven received a letter purporting to be from the 'real' killer of Mr Goodman:

So you believe in your husband – so do i. I'm the only bloke who nos the facts, I'll tell you all about it, but this wont help him any as he'll hang like a man –him – not me....don't take this to the cops as they wont help you any, the thick nuts thinks he did it and you wont turn them from their duty.

The letter ends with the farewell: 'good-by, until he is strung up and after. My name is – ? aint I wide.' This curious document contains details of the killing which were known only to the family and friends of Raven and, in all probability, originated from that quarter. The police refused to take it seriously.

Despite an appeal being heard on 20 December and a petition for clemency containing 15,000 signatures, Raven was hanged at Pentonville Prison on Friday, 6 January 1950. No explanation for his actions was ever aired, either before or during his trial. However, an internal police report prepared after the execution stated that it was felt, within the force, that Raven had overtaken the Goodmans between East Finchley and Edgware, had entered into their house in order to divest them of their money and had seriously miscalculated their arrival time. Caught in highly compromising circumstances Raven had lashed out rather than face the shame and legal consequences of simple burglary. While this is plausible, we will never know for certain what went on in the mind of Daniel Raven on that night in October 1949.

CHAPTER 23

A Doctor Dies in Colindale

1957

What the doctor told me is that which made me kill him.

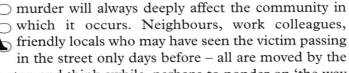 murder will always deeply affect the community in which it occurs. Neighbours, work colleagues, friendly locals who may have seen the victim passing in the street only days before – all are moved by the event to stop and think awhile, perhaps to ponder on 'the way things are going in the world today.' If the victim was popular in the community, and helpful and kind to those around them, many will be moved to leave flowers at the site of the killing, or outside the victim's home, their hearts torn by the appalling act which is murder.

Doctor Johannes Pulfer was just such a popular figure. Having escaped from Nazi Germany in 1933, the Jewish doctor came to live in Britain and, in 1939, had founded a medical practice in Sheaveshill Avenue, Colindale. Doctor Pulfer worked hard to establish himself in the area, and his generosity and kindness of spirit led to his becoming deeply popular both with his patients and in Colindale generally. He often worked far beyond official surgery hours treating the ill, or offering his counsel to the distressed, and it was said of him that he never turned anyone away. It is sad therefore that his untimely death resulted precisely from this willingness to put himself out for others.

In 1957 Doctor Pulfer had started treating a young Cypriot man, Elias Georgiou, an employee at the Phoenix Telephone Works, close to the surgery. Twenty-five-year-old Georgiou began making repeated visits to the doctor, complaining of the symptoms of an illness, evidence of which the doctor was never able to find any trace.

It was late in the evening of Tuesday, 26 March, when Georgiou made his final visit to the doctor. Pulfer had a busy social life and on that particular evening he and his wife were entertaining a couple of friends. Georgiou's visit interupted Doctor Pulfer's social engagement however, and Mrs Pulfer and the guests chatted upstairs while the doctor attended to his business. Suddenly, at about ten, his wife heard a disturbance downstairs. There was the sound of scuffling and then a cry followed by a loud crash. Rushing down the stairs and into the treatment room, she found her husband lying on his back on the floor. He was saturated with blood, his throat torn open. Standing over him was a young man with curly black hair who brandished a stiletto knife at her.

The Pulfers had a telephone in the house but this was not the time to use it; Mrs Pulfer ran screaming out into the street, heading for the junction of Sheaveshill Avenue and Colindeep Lane, intending to phone for help from a public telephone box located there. The knifeman followed her out of the house so she ran beyond the phone box, desperately seeking help from any passer-by she might stumble upon. At some point the knifeman gave up the chase and, having phoned the police from a house nearby, the distraught Mrs Pulfer was picked up in a matter of minutes by a police car acting on the emergency call.

In the meantime the guests had tended the badly wounded doctor. He had remained alive for a few moments following the attack, but by the time his wife returned to the house with the police he had expired. A murder inquiry was immediately begun and, as horrified neighbours crowded outside the suburban house, the street filled with police cars and motorcycles.

Detective Superintendent Leonard Crawford, head of S Division CID, arrived to take charge of the inquiry. Joe, a well-known police dog who had been employed in the search for terrorist devices in Cyprus the previous year, together with his handler, PC Charles Lindeburn, joined a large group of officers in a search of the surrounding area for the murder weapon.

It was quickly learned that a man answering to the description of the assailant had been seen running into

Colindale underground station, where he'd bought a ticket for a southbound train. Stations along the line were alerted and police officers placed at every stop, yet the wanted man managed somehow to slip through the net and escape.

Within minutes the Doctor's appointments book had been studied and the finger of suspicion was pointing at Elias Georgiou. A warrant was immediately issued for his arrest. Police officers visited his flat in Highbury but found he hadn't been home. A lookout was therefore placed both at his address and at his parents' home nearby.

Throughout the next two days the police made a thorough search of Colindale Open Space and the banks of the Silkstream – the area around the doctor's house – for the weapon used. But in spite of this effort it was a worker at the Hendon Titanine factory who found the double-edged, ten-inch stiletto, hidden in a hedge opposite the surgery. Fingerprints were taken from the weapon which further verified the police's suspicions.

Two days after the killing, Georgiou was arrested at the door of his parents' home, and immediately driven to Hendon Police Station where he was seen by Detective Superintendent Crawford. Georgiou's English was weak, so an interpreter had to be supplied to assist in the interview. Georgiou initially refused to answer any of Crawford's questions, but finally agreed to make a statement, in which he admitted to the killing. After being formally charged with the murder of Doctor Pulfer, Georgiou commented: 'What the doctor told me is that which made me kill him.'

The following morning Georgiou appeared before the magistrates at Harrow Court. The chairman of the bench, T N Graham, expressed concern over whether the defendant was able to understand the proceedings, but was assured by the clerk of the court that an interpreter was available for the hearing. The police produced evidence of identity and circumstance, and Georgiou was remanded in custody for a week.

The inquest was opened at the Hendon Town Hall before the deputy coroner W R Heddy, on 2 April. Dr D G Rushton, the pathologist assigned to the case, reported that the cause of

Dr Pulfer's death was haemorrhage due to a cut throat, and stab wounds to the chest. Dr Pulfer's cousin, Rudolf Bamberger, gave evidence of identification. Mrs Pulfer was not present at the inquest, which was adjourned until 4 June.

Controversy surrounded Georgiou's final appearance at Harrow Court, when the public and press were excluded from the hearing following concerns expressed by his solicitor R Gavin Freeman. Detective Superintendent Crawford had barely begun to read from Georgiou's statement before Freeman was on his feet and raising an objection. Georgiou's statement was inadmissible as evidence, the solicitor contended. He reminded the court about comments made by a judge at a recent high profile trial – that of Dr Bodkin Adams for murder – regarding publicity following the reading of a statement in the pre-trial hearing. The statement had been widely reported by the press prior to the jury trial, and the judge had felt concerned that the jury had therefore been rendered incapable of forming an objective view of that same evidence when it had been presented in his court. Freeman then asked the magistrate to exclude the press from the proceedings forthwith; pointing out that it was entirely in the power of the court to do so. After some debate this was indeed agreed to, and the various members of the press had to wait in the foyer outside the courtroom, only learning of the outcome of the hearing from the mouth of the clerk himself. Georgiou had been committed for trial at the Old Bailey, and had been granted a defence certificate for two counsel, in view of the seriousness of the offence.

The trial took place in Court Number One at the Old Bailey on Wednesday, 10 May before Mr Justice Gorman. Christmas Humphreys, acting for the Crown, stated immediately that there was a preliminary matter to be decided by the jury, this being whether the accused was fit to plea. Dr Matheson, from Brixton Prison, was called to give evidence, and told the court that Georgiou was suffering from paranoid schizophrenia and that he was subject to severe delusions of the mind and occasional outbursts of violence. The jury was sworn in: they then discussed the facts presented, and concluded that Georgiou was unfit to plead, Justice Gorman thereupon committing the prisoner to a secure hospital.

The following week the *Hendon and Finchley Times* ran an article testifying to Doctor Pulfer's selfless service to his community. Among the quotes from friends and acquaintances used was one taken from a letter sent by a seven-year-old boy to Mrs Pulfer, following the tragedy. He had been presented with a gift, a game of Scrabble, by the late doctor and, remembering the kind act, had felt moved to write:

Dear Auntie:

How are you? I think you must be feeling very miserable. I am feeling very miserable too. I suppose you are feeling more miserable than I am. I loved Uncle Hannes very much and I will look after my game of Scrabble because he gave it to me.

We should note that the young man was a relative of neither Dr nor Mrs Pulfer's, the words 'Auntie' and 'Uncle' being indicative of the depths to which the good doctor's works had touched those around him.

CHAPTER 24

The Girl in the Dollis Brook

1959

I am sorry now, but that won't give her life back.

n March 1957, the Homicide Act was passed in Parliament. The death penalty was now only to be exacted for five types of murder:

- Murder committed in the course of furtherance of theft
- Murder caused by shooting or by an explosion
- Murder in the course of, or for the purpose of, resisting or avoiding or preventing a lawful arrest
- Murder of a police officer acting in the execution of his duty, or a person so assisting him
- Murder of a prison officer or murder done by a prisoner

So, given the timing, the perpetrator in the case described below was, perhaps, singularly lucky with respect to the change in the law: two or three years' earlier he would have been sentenced to death for what was a coldly calculated killing.

Nineteen-year-old Miriam Anne Young (or *von* Young to use her full name) was a popular young woman who lived with her parents in Hendon Lane. She was described by her father as 'a very quiet girl, neat and clean.' Miriam had been educated at the Convent of Marie Auxiliarice, sited in the Finchley Manor House in East End Road, and regularly attended Ballards Lane Methodist Church in North Finchley. She enjoyed going to dances in Totteridge and playing the guitar. Recently, she had begun a secretarial course at the St Godric's College, a secretarial school in Hampstead. A photograph printed in the

Kemp Hall, Totteridge, 1948. LBB

Hendon and Finchley Times at the time shows an attractive curly haired woman who, presumably, had no shortage of potential suitors.

At some time in 1958 Miriam befriended Hubert James Dughard, twenty-one, a plastics worker from Muswell Hill. For a while they went out together, often enjoying Saturday night 'hops' at Kemp Hall on Totteridge Common, and seem to have been 'an item'. Certainly that was Dughard's interpretation of events. At Christmas 1958 Miriam sent him what was later described in court as an 'affectionate' seasonal card. However, by July 1959 Young was indicating she wanted to break off their friendship. She had also started going out with a French student named Allen who was staying in the family home – or so she claimed. She wrote to Dughard on 15 July expressing her wishes and they agreed to meet once more to say farewell.

It was in the early hours of Monday, 20 July that the police station at Golders Green received a startling report from the Muswell Hill station. According to information received, there was the likelihood that the body of a young woman would be found in the Dollis Brook. Detective Superintendent Shepherd and Detective Inspector Hoggins of the Finchley and Golders Green CID raced through the streets of Hendon to the place described; a shallow part of the brook, alongside the footpath towards Bell Lane from close to the junction of the Great North Way and Hendon Lane. According to descriptions of the place dating from the time, it was a well-loved beauty spot, popular with courting couples.

Making their way along the side of the brook by torch-light, the officers peered into the darkness – hoping, perhaps, that the exercise was futile and that they had been sent on a fool's errand, but it was not to be. About fifty yards from the entrance to the brook, alongside an island formed by a temporary splitting of the stream, they came across a body lying in the water.

Support was summoned and the corpse hauled onto the bank of the brook with the aid of a rope. An adventurous officer, PC Belcher, removed his trousers before wading into the water in his shirt and socks to retrieve a black and white check box-style handbag bobbing up and down in the current. The body was that of a young woman; she was dressed in a white blouse and a red skirt, which had ridden above her head due to the action of the water. Wound tightly around the girl's neck was a ligature, from which a yard or so of spare rope extended. Her wristwatch had stopped at 10.45. After an examination by the police surgeon, Dr Mathews, the body was taken to Finchley mortuary and a murder inquiry opened.

Shortly before midnight on the previous night, Desmond Watt, a mutual friend of Miriam Young and Dughard, was sitting in his flat in Curzon Road, Muswell Hill. He was about to turn in after attending a dance when he heard an unexpected knock at his door. He opened it to find a distraught Dughard standing before him. 'I have done in Miriam,' Dughard blurted out. 'She broke my heart and kept tormenting me about the French boy she has been out with. I

The site of the murder, Dollis Brook, 2007. The author

lost control of myself.' Dughard asked for a cup of tea and then said that he intended to hand himself in to the authorities. He asked his friend to accompany him, and this Watt agreed to do.

Police Sergeant Hamilton was working a late shift at Muswell Hill Police Station. At about one-thirty on Monday morning Dughard, accompanied by Desmond Watt, entered the station and approached him. Dughard said 'I have just killed my girl friend and put her in Dollis Brook, near Henly's Corner.'

Dughard was immediately cautioned and detained, and a message sent to Golders Green, as we have seen. Several hours later, after Miriam Young's body had been found, Dughard was interviewed by Detectives Shepherd and Hoggins before being removed to Golders Green Police Station. Here he made a statement admitting to the murder.

The next morning Dughard appeared at Highgate Court. He was clearly distraught and had to be supported by two police officers while in the dock. The accused was granted

Dughard is driven from court. Getty Images

legal aid before being remanded in custody until 29 July. He was helped from the dock, weeping, and driven away in a grey saloon car.

At about the same time the victim's father, Hans Joachim von Young, prostrate with grief, positively identified the body. Miriam Young had failed to return home the previous night, and he had gone to bed as usual. Early the next morning the police had called to tell him the sad news, and he accompanied them to the mortuary. He told the police that he knew Dughard as a friend of his daughter, and that Dughard had visited the family home several times in the past.

The post-mortem, carried out by Dr Donald Rushton, of Kings College Hospital, two days later confirmed a ligature around the victim's neck, with deep abrasions to the skin. The cord used was found later to have been cut from a clothesline in the garden at Dughard's house in Roseberry Avenue, Muswell Hill. Death was due to strangulation, not drowning.

Dr A P L Cogswell headed the inquest, which was held at Hendon Town Hall on 30 July. The victim's father formally identified the body and evidence as to cause of death was presented by Dr Rushton. Dughard was represented by his solicitor, Mr J Hugh Jones. The inquest was adjourned until 1 October.

On the following day over sixty mourners joined the visibly distraught parents in a service at the Finchley Methodist Church, where the minister, the Reverend Leslie Gray, gave an address. He asked the congregation to pray and ask forgiveness for 'the one who has done this terrible deed.' Six nuns joined the mourners at the burial in the St Marylebone cemetery, and consoled Mrs von Young who was in a state of near-collapse.

Great interest was shown in the case; the *Evening Standard* published a photograph of the accused leaving court. Several newspapers inadvertently published a picture purporting to be of the victim – it was in fact a photograph of a well-known society heiress.

In the meantime, the police had been busy assembling evidence of the events leading up to the killing. It was known that Miriam Young had spent most of the Sunday with a friend, Peter Jameson, at his home in Walmington Fold, Finchley. At about seven in the evening he drove Miriam Young to West Finchley underground station where she boarded a train in the direction of town. She had seemed perfectly happy and was carrying the check box-bag found later at the scene of crime.

The police relied heavily on the statement which Dughard had made on the morning following the murder. According to him, he had met Miriam Young by arrangement at East Finchley tube station at 7.30 pm and they travelled together to Tottenham Court Road. They went into Soho and sat in a coffee bar for an hour or so, drinking cola and discussing their break-up.

Later, they travelled back by tube to Golders Green and took a bus to Hendon Quadrant. Dughard offered to walk Miriam Young back to her house in Hendon Lane and they set off down Finchley Lane on foot. As they came to the low-point in the road – where the lane crosses both the Great North Way and Dollis Brook, before changing its name to Hendon Lane – Dughard suggested they take a short walk along the footpath beside the brook. She agreed to this and they set off together. According to Dughard, Miriam Young started mocking him about the French boy, Allen. He then lost all control of himself: 'I put the rope around her neck and pulled it. All I heard was two screams and then she fell down and collapsed to the ground. So I dumped her in the water.'

Any mitigation that Dughard hoped to gain from the suggestion of provocation on Miriam Young's part is seriously undermined by his next admission: the length of rope that he used was cut from his washing line that morning; Dughard had carried it with him throughout the day. Further, he admitted to showing Miriam Young the rope earlier in the evening and had told her that he intended to kill her. Presumably his victim-to-be had dismissed this as mere immature posturing on his part. As mentioned, the rope found around Miriam Young's neck had been analysed and was identical in texture and size to a washing line collected from the garden of Dughard's flat.

The boy Allen was questioned about his relationship with Miriam Young. He denied adamantly having had anything other than a casual friendship with her, and it seems likely that Miriam Young used his name as a device, either to justify the break-up with Dughard, or to force him to work harder in their relationship. Certainly that was the view later taken by the investigating officers.

Dughard appeared at Highgate Court on 29 July and was remanded until 6 August when, it was intimated, the police would be ready to proceed with the case. In the meantime, the various witness statements were scrutinised by the Director of Public Prosecutions, with the result that when Dughard next appeared at Highgate he was committed to trial at the Central Criminal Court.

The case came to trial at the Old Bailey on 24 October before Justice Edmund Davies: it lasted a mere ten minutes. Dughard pleaded guilty to the murder and was sentenced to life imprisonment. Prior to sentence, Counsel told the court that Dughard had said: 'I cannot undo what has now been done. The reason I killed her was I didn't want to lose her. I am sorry now, but that won't give her life back.'

Dughard filed an appeal but was refused a hearing, probably because he appealed against both prosecution and sentence. The application, held in the The National Archives at Kew is a curiously ill-focussed document. The prisoner seems to feel that appealing to the sentiments of the authorities would be sufficient in itself. One excerpt is particularly revealing: in a sort of essay entitled 'My Story and What Happened' Dughard claims once more that Miriam Young tormented him on the night of the murder about the French boy Allen. He ends: 'I never, on no account had the intention of killing her, as Miriam meant the world to me and I loved her very deeply, but it happened.'

Sources

A wide variety of sources has been drawn on for the material in this book:

First and foremost must be the large collection of back copies of the *Hendon and Finchley Times* stored at the London Borough of Barnet's local studies archive at Daws Lane, Mill Hill and at the British Library's newspaper archive in Colindale.

Copies of the *Finchley Press* and the *Barnet Press* were also viewed at Daws Lane, while the articles on Brian Donald Hume published in the *Sunday Pictorial* were studied closely at Colindale.

The Times on-line is viewable free of charge to Barnet library users as part of the '24/7' reference library service and this provided additional information on the cases covered in these pages.

Last, but not least, several visits to The National Archives at Kew allowed me to read back on police reports, inquiry forms and intelligence assessments and court transcripts of many of the murders contained herein.

A small selection of books proved their worth during the writing of this work. These included:

Middlesex County Records (old series) vol. 1, HMSO, 1972, edited by Jeaffreson, JC.

Koestler, A, Rolph, C H, *Hanged by the Neck*, Penguin, 1961.

Nature Conversation in Barnet – Ecology Handbook 28, London Ecology Unit, 1997.

The Concise Encyclopaedia of Crime and Criminals, Bookplan, undated, edited by Scott, Sir Harold.

Biggers, JR, *Finchley and Neighbourhood*, 1903.

Where to Live Around London (Northern Side), The Homeland Association, 1906.

Finally, my trusty old friend, the *Reference Atlas of Greater London (Extended Edition)*, Bartholemew, 1957, provided me with details on the layout of each site within which the individual killings took place.

Many of the photographs used I took myself. However, Peter Simon provided me with some choice specimens taken during long walks we took together. The *Hendon and Finchley Times* allowed me to use their photograph of Ernest Walter Smee. Yasmine Webb and Hugh Petrie at Daws Lane helped me select a few good pictures from the Barnet archive. Will Self kindly purchased the photograph of James Hubert Dughard from Getty Images and presented it to me as a present on the occasion of my fiftieth birthday!

Index

Aeroville 76
Aggis, Leonard 69–71
Alverstone, Lord 49
Andrews, Detective Inspector 110
Armitage Mansions 88
Armstrong, John 118, 121
Ashby, Dr JE 134, 140
Ashcombe Gardens 168–174
Austin, Harry 62, 63
Ayres, Herbert ('Pigsticker')
118–122

Baker, John 28–31
Bald Faced Stag, The (Burnt Oak)
45, 46,
Bald Faced Stag, The (East
Finchley) 26, 27
Ballards Lane 155, 182
Bamberger, Rudolf 180
Barfoot, Arthur Henry 126–132
Barnet, London Borough of 6, 32,
144
Barnet Way 145
Barrel, Divisional Inspector 71
Battershill, PC 45
Bell Lane 184
Belcher, PC 184
Bennett, Divisional Detective
Inspector 110, 116, 118–120
Bethune, Dr 70, 71
Beveridge, Detective
Superintendent Peter 170–173
Biggin, Arthur John 76–85
Birch, Inspector 147
Birkett, Norman, KC 102
Bodkin, WP 29
Boot, The 121
Brent Cross 7, 86
Brent, River 86, 89, 93
Brentmead Place 87
Brinkley, Walter & James 26, 28
Brixton Prison 35, 48, 59, 93,
97,137, 180
Broadfields Avenue 133–137
Bronte, Dr RM 111
Brooke, Detective Inspector Henry
55–57, 65
Buxted Road, 99 100

Camps, Dr Francis 159
Carr, John 52–57
Cassells, Mr Justice 174, 175
Central London Sick Asylum 68
Cherrill, Superintendent 147
Child, John 10, 145–152
Churchill, John & Robert 44
Clarke, Enoch 25–31
Clay Lane 8, 115–123, 133
Cogswell, Dr APL 186
Cohen, George 12, 57, 64, 71, 75,
81, 94, 130, 148
Colindale Avenue 77–80

Colindale Open Space 179
Colindale Underground Station
179
Colindeep Lane 178
College Farm, Finchley 5, 39–43
Convent of Marie Auxiliarice, The
182
Cook, PC 55, 94
Cooke, Dr Whitehall 46
Cooper, Herbert 61–64
Cooper, PC 80
Coppett's Wood 25–31
Cover, Thomas 22–24
Cowper, Dr William 61
Cox, Edward William 146
Cozens, Fred 122
Crawford, Detective
Superintendent Leonard
178–180
Creighton Avenue 169
Cricklewood Lane 69
Curtis Bennett, Henry 95–97

Darling, Mr Justice 59, 83, 84
Davies, Detective Inspector 161
Davies, Mr Justice Edmund 188
Davies, Leonard Ward 136–137
Davies, Station Sergeant 71
Deerfield Cottages 69, 80
Didham, Dorothy 110, 111
Diller, Detective Inspector 171,
172, 175
Dodd, Inspector (later
Superintendent) Charles 26–29,
41
Dollis Brook 182–187
Dow, Dr JR 113
Draper, Elizabeth 22–24
Driscoll, PC 134
Dughard, James Hubert 183–88

East Barnet 7, 32–34
East End Road 43, 61–63, 182
East Finchley Baby Farm Murders
The, 12
Edgware Hardware Stores 128
Edgware Police Station 109, 119,
128, 133, 140, 171
Edgwarebury Lane 115–117,
168–174
Edrick Walk 125, 130
Ellis, John 98
Elstree Aerodrome 160–167

Farm Road 125, 128
Fielde, James, Priscella & Frances
19
Finchley Common 11, 25, 26
Finchley Lane 187
Finchley Police Station
Finchley Road 39, 161–166
Finchley Urban District Council 51

Finnemore, DL 102
Fletcher, Annie Lydia 47–49, 56
Fletcher, Violet 69, 70, 71
Forum Club, The 126, 127
Fox, Rev WJ 72
Franklyn Gardens (Edgwarebury)
133
Fulton, Eustace 82, 83, 95, 98

George, Francis 16
Georgiou, Elias 177–180
Gibson, WS 48, 57
Goddard, Mr Justice 141–143
Golders Green Police Station 90,
113, 185
Golders Green Road 70, 88–89
Goodman, Mr & Mrs Leopold
168–176
Goody, Rev CJ 58
Gorman, Mr Justice 180
Gorski, Dr AM 148
Goslett, Arthur Andrew Clement
86–98, 139
Goslett, Evelyn 86–98
Grahame-White, Claude 65, 66
Grahame-White Aviation
Company, The 68
Gray, Rev Leslie 186
Great North Way, The 184, 187
Gregory, John Thomas 77–85, 144

Hammond, Dr William 106
Hand, Alice 139–142
Hanot, Francois 65–68
Hardingstone (Northamptonshire)
8, 99–101
Hart, Mr & Mrs Robert Vernon
112–114
Harte, Richard 19
Hawkins, Detective 146, 147
Hawkins, Mr Justice 30,
Haynes, Robert 16
Heddy, WR 179
Hendon Aerodrome 65–68, 76
Hendon Lane 182, 184, 187
Hendon Magistrates' Court, 122,
129, 174
Hendon Park Cemetery 68, 73,
130,
Hendon Police Court 82, 134, 141
Hendon Police Station 82, 179
Hendon Quadrant 187
Hendon Town Hall 47, 71, 81, 93,
114, 117, 130, 148, 179, 186
Hendon Union Workhouse 45
Hendon Urban District Council 7
Hendon Way 7
Hickling 125–132, 138
Hill, Lydia 32–38
Hoggins, Detective Inspector 184,
185
Holloway Prison 12, 135

Holt, Daisy 90–97
Homicide Act (1957), The 182
Houghton, Ralph 15
Hume, Brian Donald 158–189
Humphreys, Mr Justice Travers 131, 135
Humphreys, Christmas 142, 165, 180
Hutchinson, St John 142–143

Integral Propeller Company 76

Jackson, Arthur 62, 63
Jenkins, Ivy 99
Jenkins, Phyllis 100
'Joe' (police dog) 178

Kemp Hall (Totteridge) 183
Kemp's Biscuit Factory (West Hendon) 125
Kings College Hospital 186

Lancaster Road 32, 34, 35
Lewis, Mr Justice 165
Lewys, Hugh 15
Linford, Alice Isabel 52–58
Ling, Mrs 155, 156
Little Atom Electrical Products 164
Long Street (Longmore Avenue, East Barnet) 32
Luxmore-Drew, C 75
Luxton, Sergeant 71, 80
Lyon, William 19

MacDougall, Superintendent 159–163
Mant, Barbara 125–132
Matheson, Dr 180
McClure, G 141, 142
McGlade, Michael 115, 116
McKie, William 72
Melrose Avenue 45
Metropolitan Electric Tramway Company 54, 58
Middlesex County Council 12, 13
Miller, Agnes 19
Mitchell, Jesse & Jean, 133–136, 142
Moat Mount, 115, 145–153
Moore, Alan 104
Moriarty, Dr 108–111
Morrison, Dr Walter 106
Muir, Sir Richard 83, 95

Nan Clark 9, 150
Narborough, Inspector F 134, 135
Neil, Chief Detective Inspector 80–82, 88–96
New Edgware 108
Newman Oliver ('Tiggy') 8, 118–122, 133
Nieuport Aircraft Works 96
Nilsen, Denis Andrew 45
North Circular Road, The 26, 70, 86, 87
Norton, Freman 16

Old Bailey, The 14, 30, 83, 95, 112, 122, 131, 135, 137, 156, 164,174, 180, 188
Orange Tree, The 42
Osborn, Thomas 34–38

Park Farm 61–64
Pateman, George Baron 12, 52–59
Penshurst Gardens 108
Pentonville Prison 98, 122, 175
Petit Pierre, Maurice 66–68
Phoenix Telephone Works 177
Pickett, Detective Sergeant 116–120
Pierrepont, Albert 103
Pierrepont, Thomas William 103
Poole, Geoffrey 15
Prescelly Place 138–141
Prince Albert, The 69, 92
Prince of Wales, The 32
Prospect Road 45
Pulfer, Dr Johannes 177–181
Pymme's Brook 32

Railway Hotel, The 126, 127
Raven, Daniel 168–176
Ravenscroft Gardens 113
Red Lion, The 38
Redhill Hospital 12, 109, 114, 140
Regents Parade 54
Rising Sun, The 149
Ritz, The (cinema) 124–129
Rouse, Alfred Arthur 8, 99–104, 142
Rushton, Dr DG 179
Russell, Grace 113
Rutter, Elizabeth 1, 19
Rutter, S 17
Ryan, Michael 151–153

St John's Parade, West Hendon 73
St Marylebone Cemetery 43, 63, 186
St Mary's Church, Hendon 73
St Mary's Hospital 35, 58, 68, 75
Sach, Amelia 12
Sanger, 'Lord' George 56, 60–64
Saunders Garage 163, 164
Saunders, Richard 121, 122
Savage, Superintendent 116
Seaman, Edwin 16
Sellars, Mr Justice 165
Semken, Mrs, 108 110
'Serum Test' 190
Setty, Stanley 158–166
Shaw, Dr Holgate 87, 94
Shearman, Mr Justice 95–98
Sheaveshill Avenue 177, 178
Shelley, William ('Moosh') 8, 118–122, 133
Sherring, Albert 68–73
Sherring Beatrice 68–73
SilkStream, 5, 45–50 179
Simpson, Herbert 160
Simpson, Dr Keith 114
Skelly, Detective Sergeant 101

Smale, Detective Inspector John 113
Smee, Ernest Walter 8, 138–143
Spash, Divisional Detective Inspector 130, 134, 140
Spencer, Mary 105–107
Spilsbury, (Sir) Bernard 56, 94, 102, 117, 148
Spotted Dog, The 45
Stanhope Road 155
Stanley Road 74
Suicide (including attempted) 10, 21, 41, 59, 60, 64, 68, 73, 75, 105, 134 Sutherland, Detective Sergeant 159
Swan & Pyramid, The 101
Swift, Mr Justice 122

Talbot, Mr Justice 102
Tansill, Detective Chief Inspector Albert 172
Taylor, Edward 98
Terriss, William 40
Thomas, Dr Danford 12, 27, 42, 49, 68
Three Cups of Coffee, The 35
Tiffin, Sydney 158, 159
Titanine Works (Hendon) 80, 179
Toogood, Dr Frederick 97
Tottenham Court Road Underground Station 8, 78, 80, 136, 187
Totterhall, Detective Inspector 159, 160
Tucker, Nellie 100
Tuke, Iva 108, 111
Tuke, Thomas 108
Tuke, William Clarence 108–112

Vespor, Samuel 173

Walmington Fold (Finchley) 187
Walrond, Charles 16
Watt, Desmond 184–185
Warwick Tavern, The 35
Waters, Annie 12
Waters, Avril Ray 8, 136–137
Watford By-pass 107, 115, 119, 137, 168, 170
Webb, Thomas 39–44
Welshe, Edward 15
West, Charles Edmund 73–75
West Finchley Underground Station 187
West Hendon Broadway 73–74
West Hendon Baptist Hall 72
Western Avenue 86, 92, 93
Whetstone High Road 99
Wilberforce Road 69–73
Wilcox, Dr William Henry 58
Wixen, PC 109
Woodside Avenue 51–54

Young, Hans Joachim *von* 186
Young, Miriam *von*, 6 182–188